COMMUNICATION OPPORTUNITIES

Ronald Howell

Illinois Central College

Kendall Hunt
publishing company

Kendall Hunt
publishing company

www.kendallhunt.com
Send all inquiries to:
4050 Westmark Drive
Dubuque, IA 52004-1840

Contents

Beyond Aristotle

The opportunity for successful communication (especially face-to-face communication) is a terrible thing to waste. Humans have a need to communicate. Communication is the only tool that links one person to another person. If communication is extracted from the equation, total isolation is the result. Imagine never being able to express your thoughts, your feelings, your needs, your desires, your opinions, and your reactions to another person. It has been said that communication is a part of all we have been, all we are, and all that we will be. Effective communication skills can help you get the job, keep the job, get the raise, and lead a happier interpersonal life. Since communication is such a critical factor in human existence, studying and better understanding it should help you improve your communication skills. This in turn will improve your life.

Studying communication is not the same as studying public speaking, but public speaking is a part of almost any general study of communication. The ability to speak well in public is a wonderful skill, but formal public speaking is only a fraction of the whole communication picture. Most people spend much more time communicating outside the speaker-audience situation. Thus, an examination of human communication must contain

more than instruction in public speaking. How should an effective study of communication be organized? Perhaps the best way to approach the study of communication is to first understand the goal of this endeavor. Even though his focus was on public speaking, Aristotle, a philosopher and rhetorician from ancient Greece, provides one of the finest explanations of what studying communication can allow the serious student to acquire.

According to Aristotle, becoming a better communicator requires the mastery of three essential tools, known by some as *ethos, pathos*, and *logos*. In terms of communication, each term requires more than a literal translation. Of the three tools, *ethos* is most vital to effective communication. A good explanation of *ethos* focuses on credibility. Few who study communication would think to begin that study by pondering the idea of credibility. So, how does credibility relate to effective communication? Among your friends and relatives, can you find three who, no matter what they told you (under normal circumstances), you would believe without question? Most people would be hard pressed to name even one person in their lives who had that much credibility. However, the opposing list should be easy to compile. Try to identify three people whose every communication you take with the proverbial grain of salt. Sometimes, when describing an event, they get the names, the events, and/or the location wrong. These people have a serious credibility problem. The critical thing to remember is that we listen more carefully and better when we can trust the communicator than when we cannot. As Aristotle intimated, lack of credibility means lack of effective communication. Of course, when most students think of studying communication, credibility is not at the top of their list of necessary skills, but now we all know differently.

Aristotle also wrote about *pathos*. The best modern translation for this term is *emotional manipulation*. When most people encounter the word *manipulation*, any definition of it seems to have a negative connotation. Some forms of manipulation do have a negative context; advertisements that play on the heart strings to achieve some sort of behavioral control may be viewed as negative. However, there are forms of manipulation that are inherently positive. For example, there is the ability to generate interest on the part of a communicator. Some communicators seem to be naturally more skilled than others in the use of emotional manipulation. Some studies indicate that as early as kindergarten, children can identify their more interesting and less interesting classmates. Let's put this in context; think of three family members and friends to whom you really enjoy listening. Ask yourself why. Now, think of three family members and acquaintances whom you instinctively try to avoid. Ask yourself why. Could it be that they are as fascinating as grass growing in real time? No person needs to be boring when communicating; it is all about learning to use *pathos*.

The final tool that Aristotle gives us is *logos*. This tool, which deals with logic and reasoning, is probably the most misused of the three essential tools. All too often, communicators interpret reasoning with another person and generating understanding as securing agreement with a point of view. This is not the case. People can understand but still disagree with a particular point of view. Trying to force agreement often gets in the way of both logic and reasoning.

Essentially, the study of communication can focus on teaching students how to better use Aristotle's three essential tools. The idea is that if they are successful in using these tools, the students will also be successful in communicating with others in both one-on-one and speaker-audience situations.

Among the things we need to do to study communication effectively is to define it, at least in part. To define communication as if we fully understood it would be misleading. Defining something doesn't always indicate full understanding. At best, defining some things is a beginning. For example, take the word *infinity*. Any competent dictionary can provide words that define infinity, but after reading those words, do you really have a full understanding of what "forever" is? Instead of providing a definition of the word *communication*, which, like the word *infinity*, encompasses so much, I shall describe some (not all) of what communication can be.

First, *communication is constantly occurring*. Humans virtually always communicate—from before birth until after death and at all points in between. Even when you are alone, if you hum, sing, or talk to yourself, you are communicating. You don't even have to talk, hum, or sing for communication to occur. The process of life itself is one of communication. Nerve synapses send and receive electrical communication; the cells of the body engage in biochemical communication. We can add dreaming to the list. As we dream, the conscious and subconscious aspects of ourselves communicate with one another.

Second, *communication is constantly changing.* Have you ever had a friend with a fishing story? Did you notice that the struggle with the fish as well as the fish's size changed with every retelling of the story? Even if your friend wanted to tell the story exactly the same way each time, it would not happen. Many variables are at work that will cause the story to change. If you have ever been in a play with a speaking part, did you say your lines exactly the same way in each performance? Or did variables like the energy of the audience, the energy of the rest of the cast, the weather outside, and/or the indoor temperature have varying impacts?

Third, *communication involves an exchange.* The nerve synapses exchange electrical impulses. The cells of the body use biochemical signals to communicate. Humans use words and nonwords to express feelings and ideas to one another. Animals use a "vocabulary" of growls, snarls, whimpers, and smells to signal one another.

Fourth, *communication involves a relationship.* Human communication relationships have some unique facets. The *human communication bonding process* is the basis of human communication relationships. This process is subconsciously guided by and based primarily on nonverbal factors. During the first substantial encounter between two people, the bonding process occurs. The subconscious mind becomes a superabsorbing computer that gathers all sorts of nonverbal characteristics of the new person. Have you ever met someone for the first time who did nothing weird or unusual but still evoked, as you walked away, a strong feeling of dislike? That is the bonding process in action. Although this process produces either a positive or a negative outcome, we seem to be aware only of the strongly positive or strongly negative effect. If the result of the bond is weakly positive or weakly negative, humans are likely to interpret it as neutral. Our reactions to people are almost never neutral. Where do those reactions come from? They come from our past experiences with people. Something as simple as a vocal quality, smell, or shape can trigger a tiny cascade of memories that impact present behavior. In other words, we want to relate to the new person as we did to the one of whom he or she reminds us.

In reality there are four, as opposed to two, possible bonds: true positive, true negative, false negative, and false positive. The true positive bond means that the positive characteristics that we thought the new person had actually existed. The new person had those and other positive characteristics. To put it bluntly, we liked the new person, and he or she gave us reasons to do so. The true negative bond is also correct. We associated the new person with negative characteristics that we have experienced in other people, and as it turns out, the new person has those or other negative characteristics. We did not like the person, and he or she will give us continued reasons not to do so.

The false negative and false positive bonds occur when we get it wrong. A false negative bond means that we have made an incorrect association between the negative experiences with people in the past and the new person. In other words, we do not like the new person, but the person does not reinforce our dislike. Don't get excited just yet. First, it will take us some time to get past our initial negative reaction. Even then, there will be a limit to how closely we can bond with the new person. One likely outcome is that our egocentric nature takes over. We want to be right, so we wait for the new person to make a mistake that will justify our dislike. The most potentially deadly outcome of the human communication bonding process is the false positive bond. Think about what could happen if you associate a new person with positive characteristics from your past that this person doesn't have. In fact, the new person may have few or no positive characteristics. If you add that reaction to your egocentric nature, you have a recipe for disaster. We meet someone and strongly like this person because he or she possesses (we think) all of the wonderful characteristics embodied in people from our past. Even if this person treats us badly (depending on the strength of the bond), some of us will continue the relationship because we need to validate those positive characteristics that we thought existed. Could this be one basis for an abusive relationship? Children have to be taught not to go to strangers because a child's storehouse of people knowledge is mostly positive. Family and friends all represent positive characteristics. As we grow older, our storehouse of negative human characteristics gets larger, and we are less likely to draw only from the positive pool. First impressions do count. What happens when you are in a job interview and bond negatively with the interviewer because you are a reminder of someone who used to to torture him or her in the third grade?

© Phase4Photography, 2009. Used under license from Shutterstock, Inc.

Fifth, *communication is heavily influenced by culture and coculture.* For our purposes, let's define *culture* as the attitudes, beliefs, values, and behaviors characteristic of a group of people who reside in the same country and/or region of the world. Can you think of attitudes, beliefs, values, and behaviors that are common to the American culture? How about North America? A *coculture* is defined as a group or groups within a culture who have attitudes, beliefs, behaviors, and values that differ from those of the group as a whole. Some examples of cocultural groups include those defined by gender, race, religion, age, and region.

Sixth, *communication is power.* Many studies conclude that people with better communication skills get hired faster, get promoted quicker, and lead happier interpersonal lives. However, the fact that communication is power is not a new lesson for most persons. Let's go back to the very first day of your life. You probably do not have vivid memories of that time, but since there is a commonality among human infants, we can generalize.

© Bettmann/Corbis

When you first experienced hunger after being born, you couldn't run down to the hospital cafeteria and grab a snack. You were helpless. In frustration, you cried, and someone made sure that you got the food you needed. Very early on, then, you recognized that communicating could get you what you wanted and exert influence over people. When your diaper was dirty, you cried to get it changed. When you were bored, you cried until someone sang for you, made funny faces for you, and/or bounced you on his or her knee. Toddlers are powerful enough to take over the world, but they don't know it. Toddlers can persuade you to give them cookies and candy because they are so cute. If they were a bit more sophisticated, they would ask for deeds to property and keys to the safety deposit box instead of cookies and candy. And who could forget the student in high school who never did homework or papers on time but always had the right sob story that led to an extension of the deadline? Thus, we can conclude that the better your communication skills, the more influence you can exert over others and the greater your power.

Finally, *communication is a process*. It requires a series of steps that should occur in a particular order. Communication isn't as simple as some might think. There is much more to it than simply directing your words to someone else's ears. That process requires an extensive discussion of its own.

The Process of Communication

There are many different communication forms, and each has its place. A story was told to me by a former student involving the student's brother and his brother's girlfriend. The brother and his girlfriend were sitting on a sofa (inches from one another) and texting their conversation. There was no noise or other people in the house to merit the use of this communication form. Using text messaging, the brother proposed to his girlfriend and, using text messaging, she accepted. For some people, face-to-face communication seems to be a challenge. Perhaps if the *process* of communication is better understood, the fear of face-to-face communication will diminish.

To understand the process of communication, let's examine a dyadic (two-person) communication situation.

When there is something that you wish to communicate to another person and you start the process, you are called the *source/encoder*. The source aspect means that you started the communication process, and the encoder portion means that you took the thoughts/word pictures in your mind and converted them into words and nonwords so that the other person could understand them.

As the source/encoder, you are responsible for a very important decision: the level of communication. Your communication could emphasize any of the following levels: intrapersonal, interpersonal, mass, group, intercultural, and/or metacommunication.

- *Intrapersonal communication* involves only one person. It can be called *communication with the self,* and it often involves a conscious choice not to share thoughts or feelings with another. Human thought is likely the most common form of intrapersonal communication; dreaming is another form it might take.

- *Interpersonal communication* means that thoughts and feelings are shared with at least one other person. Therefore, it involves two or more people. A conversation with a friend, an acquaintance, or a family member is an example of this form of communication.

- *Mass communication* involves nonhuman as well as human communication forms. It could include a radio broadcast, a television broadcast, a twitter broadcast, a newspaper article, or a magazine story. It would be hard to confuse these types of mass communication with the human form, which involves one person speaking live to a large number of people. So, how can you tell whether a message from a live speaker is meant for mass communication or interpersonal communication? If the time available and the size of the group allow for immediate exchanges and parity or near parity of exchanges between the group and the speaker, you have interpersonal communication. If the time available and the size of the group preclude immediate exchanges and parity or near parity of exchanges, you have mass communication.

- *Group communication* has elements of interpersonal and (sometimes) mass communication. As with interpersonal communication, the key to good group relationships is interdependence. The knowledge that you can count on group members to work with you on the task at hand is important to an effective group. In fact, the degree of interdependence should be closer to that of a family unit than to that of mere friends or acquaintances. On the other hand, as in mass communication, there won't always be parity in communication exchanges.

© Yuri Arcurs, 2009. Used under license from Shutterstock, Inc.

- *Intercultural communication* overlaps with just about every other form of communication. Intercultural communication involves an exchange with persons of a different culture or coculture. For us, the term *culture* means people who live in a particular country or region of the world with attitudes, beliefs, and behaviors different from our own. For example, the United States, France, Spain, Iraq, and Great Britain each has

© Monkey Business Images, 2009. Used under license from Shutterstock, Inc.

its own culture. A coculture exists within a culture and exhibits attitudes, beliefs, and behaviors that may be slightly different from those of the culture as a whole. Within the United States, cocultures might be represented by gender, race, age, religion, physical ability, socioeconomic status, population density (rural or urban), and region. People from different cultures and cocultures will likely encode and decode communications differently. This makes the need for understanding communication more important than ever before.

- *Metacommunication* is communication of habit. It usually involves little listening and little thought. Metacommunication includes the automatic responses found in "chit-chat." An example is the greeting ritual "Hello, how are you?" The responses given don't always match the question asked because we know that we should say something but what we say doesn't seem all that important. I once worked at a college where I arrived every morning at the same time as the president. He was always filled with cheery greetings. I, not being a morning person, always managed a polite response to the statement "Good morning, how are you?" One fateful day, I started the exchange. I said, "Nice day, isn't it?" His response was, "I'm fine. How are you?" That response definitely did not match the question. I decided to try a little experiment. I let the exchanges go back to their normal routine. Then one morning, after "Hello, how are you?" I dropped the listening test bomb. In the same tone of voice, I responded, "My mother has been kidnapped by a band of Lithuanian midgets." He seemed to notice no difference between that and my standard reply "Fine. How are you?" Try the odd answer from time to time to see if the other person is really listening. Aside from the greeting ritual, another major use of metacommunication is what I call "taking a ride on the 'uh-huh' train." You're watching television, eating a bowl of ice cream, flipping through a magazine, and listening to music. A friend begins to tell you his or her tale of woe, but your only response throughout the story is "uh-huh." You're not paying much attention to what is being said; your brain seems to be trapped in a weakly executed multitasking loop. "Uh-huh, uh-huh, you poor, poor thing."

The second decision that the source encoder is responsible for is the purpose of the communication, of which there are four. One purpose of communication is to inform, that is, to exchange information (examples: "It's hot outside." "It's cold outside."). A second purpose of communication is to persuade or evoke a desired behavioral response (examples: "Buy scent X and the opposite sex will not be able to resist you!" "Vote for candidate Y and avoid higher taxes!"). A third purpose of communication is to entertain or amuse others. If you have ever told a funny joke or story at a party, your purpose was to amuse those who listened. The final purpose of communication is simply to make interpersonal contact. Humans have a need as well as a desire to communicate with others. If you place the typical human in a setting where he or she doesn't know anyone to have regular verbal commerce with, his or her use of the greeting ritual will increase. We need to hear other human responses, whether positive or negative. "Hello. How are you?"

Our next stop in terms of understanding the process of communication involves the *receiver/decoder*. This person takes the words and nonwords sent by the source/encoder and converts them into his or her word picture or understanding. Keep in mind that this is by no stretch of the imagination an exact process. What the source/encoder intended may be very different from what the receiver/decoder perceives.

Between the source/encoder and receiver/decoder, the receiver/decoder has the more difficult job initially. Listening demands mental toughness and concentration that most people cannot muster. Thus, we often listen at less than acceptable levels. There are two basic forms of listening: social listening and informational listening. Do not confuse the

ability to hear with the ability to listen. Hearing is a physiological function; listening is an active mental process with understanding as its terminal goal.

Since social listening requires a lower level of concentration, we tend to fare better with social listening than informational listening. There are four forms of social listening:

© Jurian Mosin, 2009. Used under license from Shutterstock, Inc.

- *Appreciative listening*, or listening for enjoyment, is the form where our listening abilities shine the most. Play your favorite piece of music just because you want to listen to it. Generally speaking, there will only be a 10 percent message loss. In other words, if your favorite song had exactly 100 words, you would hear 100 words but you would process only about 90 of those words to a level of understanding. Approximately a 10 percent message loss results even when we're listening just for ourselves.

- *Courteous listening* casts us as less than willing participants in the communication process. Have you ever stood in a line and had the person behind you start a conversation for no apparent reason? Though you might like to tell this person to be silent, you listen politely and may even take a gracious ride on the "uh-huh" train. You do this just to be polite. It is estimated, however, that more than half of the message is only heard; it is not listened to, that is, processed to a level of understanding.

- *Conversational listening* has us as willing participants in the process. Talking to a friend or family member is a good example. However, even in conversation, despite the fact that we began as willing participants, we get off the track. Though we may hear it all, we listen to only about half of the average conversation.

- The final social form of listening is *therapeutic/empathic listening*. You listen to a friend with a problem; a psychologist listens to a patient with a problem. Both of these situations are examples of therapeutic/empathic listening. Especially in times of crisis, having someone listen to us makes us feel better. In case you didn't guess, the speaker feels better but the listener may not. Still, listeners manage to achieve therapeutic/empathic listening above the general conversational level. Message losses may be around 30 to 35 percent.

The other type of listening is informational listening, and its purpose is to gather and store information for current and future use. Unfortunately, the average listener processes much less than he or she actually hears. Estimates place message losses as high as 80 to 90 percent. Despite our best efforts and despite help from taking notes, we must work to improve informational listening. A good informational listener knows how to discriminate the information as it comes in, as well as decide what information is and is not worth keeping. Those who have learned to discriminate and make critical storage decisions tend to be much better informational listeners than the norm.

Listening is actually a process within the process of communication. There are four steps to the listening process. The first step is hearing. Anyone who has the ability to perceive what is encoded has completed this step. However, it is the second step, known as the *attention step*, that trips up the average listener. From among all the stimuli that flood our perceptive range, we have to be able to lock onto a single stimulus and follow it through. We often cannot do this. Imagine having lunch and a conversation with a friend. Your friend is talking to you, but you keep drifting into the conversation of the people in the booth behind you. You end up with only parts of two different conversations. In a world where multitasking is becoming more common, our ability to focus fully on one communication is becoming more and more difficult. The last two steps in the process of listening are a pair. Understanding must always precede remembering. We will not be able to remember that which we do not understand. Thus, we have to make sure that we fully understand what has been communicated before we can remember it. Gaps in our understanding are filled in by the brain's use of the *closure principle*. Since the human brain hates incompleteness, it fills in what it thinks should be there to make the communication whole. Major misunderstandings can be due to the closure principle. Taking notes doesn't solve the problem either. How many times as a student have you looked at your notes, only to realize that you have no idea of what something means? That which is not understood cannot be remembered.

There are several major barriers to effective listening; let's examine a few of them.

- The physical conditions under which listening occurs can have a negative impact. A room that is too hot or too cold, a room that is too bright or too dark, or furniture that is too hard or too soft can all negatively affect the listening process.

- The casual attitude of a society that believes that hearing and listening are the same can be a barrier. So can the belief that one does not need to prepare oneself to listen.

- As noted earlier, the inability to focus fully is a barrier to effective listening.

- The inability to adapt is another barrier. That which is out of the ordinary will trigger a lower level of listening. A speaking rate substantially faster or slower than what the listener is accustomed to can have the same effect. A strong accent or dialect can also make listening levels fall.

- Self-fulfilling prophecies can adversely affect listening levels. If a listener develops a negative perception of a listening situation before it occurs, his or her listening level may fall. For example, deciding in advance that something will be boring or too hard to understand programs in lower listening levels in the expectation that the listener's assessment of the situation will be correct. Since we cannot foresee the future, these evaluations should be made after the listening experience.

- Defensive listening or self-focus is the last barrier that we examine. In most conversations, a defensive listener focuses more on his or her responses than on what is being said. Egocentric human nature makes us desire to look smooth or cool in front of others. Thus, we spend more time formulating responses than actually listening. In addition, both physical and emotional pain cause self-focus. As long as self-focus occurs, listening levels stay fairly low.

It is now time to turn our attention to the third part of the process model of communication. The *channel* is the means by which we communicate with another person. There are both internal and external communication channels. Our internal channels include the five senses: sight, sound, touch, smell, and taste. Of these channels, some, like smell and taste, are dedicated to more intimate communicative exchanges. Some kissing behaviors involve taste, which is why we have multi-million-dollar industries producing breath mints, breath spray, breath gum, and breath strips to make sure that we are "kissably fresh" at those special moments. Like taste, smell is a private channel of communication. It is often said that you should not be able to smell another person outside of a one one-foot radius. Colognes and perfumes aren't meant to communicate with everyone; they are designed for those whom you feel comfortable enough to allow within a foot of your person. Unlike the private channels of taste and smell, sight and sound are public channels that can be used in communicating with anyone. Usually, these channels are part of the normal communicative cycle. Touch is a flexible channel that can be used both for public communication (as in a handshake) and private communication (as in a hug).

External channels can be vast, including face-to-face encounters, phones, twitterings, email, and text messaging. The growth in technology has given us so many channels to choose from that we often do not adequately ponder channel choices. Sometimes we choose what seems easiest rather than what is most appropriate. Give serious thought and discussion to what might be the best way or ways to accomplish the following: announcing the death of a parent, breaking up with a girlfriend or boyfriend, or firing an employee.

The fourth part of any process model of communication is the *message*: that which we desire to impart to our communication partner. Messages may take a verbal, nonverbal, or written form. Because nonverbal elements like pitch, rate, and volume can influence the decoding of verbal messages, the need for a fuller understanding of nonverbal communication should be obvious. About 90 percent of our total communication package has a nonverbal component.

Feedback is the fifth element of most process models. Feedback can be relied upon to let us know that our message was received—at least in part. A common mistake in human communication is to use feedback as an indication of understanding. In a classroom situation, for example, imagine that the professor has just explained a fairly complicated theory. Everyone else in the room seems to have understood it, but you did not. However, it is you that the professor asks, "Do you understand?" Not wanting to appear less intelligent than your peers, like the typical student, you are apt to answer in the affirmative. We have feedback, but we do not have understanding. A listener who receives a message does not automatically understand it.

To acquire an acceptable level of understanding, we must modify most process models of communication by adding perception checks. A *perception check* is a verbal device designed to discern the level of understanding between you and your communicative partner. Perception checks can be used either by the source/encoder or by the receiver/decoder. As a source/encoder in the classroom, if I ask a student if he or she understands and the student responds in the affirmative, I ask the student to explain the concept. This will tell me very quickly whether or not an acceptable level of understanding has been reached. As a receiver/decoder in the classroom, I am often asked questions. If I am not sure what is being asked, I frame the question as a choice by saying, "Did you mean A or did you mean B?" The questioner may select one of the two or say "Neither," which means that we start again. Perception checks can help communicators reach an acceptable level of understanding. However, we may not be prone to use them because they are time-consuming. Despite all the changes in technology, communicating with another human is still a labor-intensive process. To be good at communicating with others, we have to be willing to dedicate the necessary time.

The sixth aspect of a process model of communication is the barriers. A *barrier* is anything that blocks understanding between the source/encoder and the receiver/decoder. Barriers can appear anywhere in the process of communicating. A source/encoder who is unsure of the purpose for communicating or who cannot adequately structure a message creates barriers. The listening levels of most receiver/decoders also bring barriers. The lack of a full understanding of nonverbal communication creates barriers both in the feedback and in the message. An unwillingness to abandon egocentrism generates barriers to perception checks.

The final piece in the process model is arguably the most important. That variable is the *situation*. The situation can control all of the other variables in the process of communicating. The situation determines who the source/encoders and receiver/decoders are. The situation influences the message, the feedback, and the perception checks. The situation even determines the barriers that will be present. To avoid simple communication breakdowns, a good communicator should analyze the situation along with other variables to help determine which modes of communication are appropriate.

Communication Situations: Words and Nonwords

"Are we to be the master of language or will language be our master?" Lewis Carroll posed this question in *Alice in Wonderland*, but it is also a question that we must ponder carefully.

A language is a coding system. A *code* consists of all the symbols and signals used in communication. This means that both words and nonwords are part of the language that we use to communicate. Without the coding system, it would be impossible to communicate with another person; the coding system is the only link between people.

The American English language is just a coding system, but many linguists argue that it is the one with the most variations. It may be possible for someone to grow up in the United States, speak the American English language, and be unable to communicate with all the other persons who grew up here speaking American English. Why isn't there a fully common coding system? Since language is the product of the people who use it, the greater the differences among the people using the coding system, the greater the differences in that system. As a diverse group of people, Americans have quite a diverse coding system.

Still, one might ask, why is there no fully common code? The answer is that the coding system functions both as an identifier and as a unifier. We perceive how others use words and nonwords, and that tells us whether or not they are members of one or more of our cocultural groups. Strong identification leads to strong unity as well. It is easier to communicate when we share large portions of a coding system.

Since language consists of both verbal and nonverbal codes, let's compare the two. First, verbal communication is terminal; it starts and stops. Nonverbal communication, by contrast, is a continuous process. The question of intent has to be explored. Most would agree that the majority of our verbal communication is consciously intentional, and many would also agree that our nonverbal communication quite often occurs without conscious intent.

Second, verbal communication is a single-channel process. Only the sense of hearing is needed to perceive verbal messages. By contrast, nonverbal communication is a multi-channel entity. All five senses are used. We see, hear, touch, taste, and smell nonverbally.

Finally, verbal communication has a much higher potential for deception than does nonverbal communication. At will, we can construct words so that they represent either the truth or fiction. It has been estimated that every time the average person practices deceit, that person's nonverbal communication can give him or her away. This, of course, assumes that you can tell the difference between fact and fiction. For some, the lines between the two are, at best, blurred.

Two men (Edward Sapir and Benjamin Lee Whorf) wrote and discussed ideas relating to the power of language. Many interpretations of what is called the *Sapir-Whorf hypothesis* still create controversy decades later. Rather than rehash the debate over linguistic determinism and linguistic relativity, let's move in a slightly different direction. Language has the power to create, distort, and/or destroy a person's perception of reality. Words and nonwords can affect and/or reflect our perceptions of reality.

Some people are what one would call *Sapir-Whorf hypothesis active*. On a regular basis, they intentionally use words and nonwords to affect or restructure another person's perception of reality. By contrast, *Sapir-Whorf hypothesis passive* people use words and nonwords as a reflection of the existing reality. As we discuss words and nonwords, we will come to the ideas behind the Sapir-Whorf hypothesis.

Let's first look at nonwords or the nonverbal coding system. Specifically, how do we use nonverbal communication? There are four basic functions in our use of nonverbal communication: reinforcement, denial, substitution, and regulation. An example of the reinforcement function might be raising the volume of your voice to stress a point or using three fingers to indicate the importance of three significant points. The denial function takes us back to the ideas of intentional and nonintentional nonverbal communication. If, for example, you ask a friend for a favor and that friend answers verbally in the affirmative while responding with a head shake in the negative, then the true response is that the friend probably does not want to do the favor. Sometimes the use of the denial function is intentional, as in the case of sarcasm, but more likely the denial function is the nonverbal truth slipping past the verbal guise. If you have ever played charades, you have used nonverbal substitution. Here the communication is through nonwords rather than through words. Without a set nonverbal alphabet and vocabulary, the substitution function has limited usefulness because there are so many possible interpretations. Something as simple as a wave of the hand could mean "hello" or it could mean "goodbye." It could mean that one person wants to talk to the other, or it could mean the opposite. It could even mean "Watch out because you are about to step in front of a bus." Lastly, we use the nonverbal coding system to regulate the flow of verbal conversation. The rate of speech, the use of pauses, and the use of silence are examples of how we keep the flow of conversation fairly smooth without being awkward. We also use the regulation function to punctuate our verbal sentences. We can use the comma, the exclamation point, and the question mark by employing the regulatory function of nonverbal communication.

Although there are many nonverbal areas to be considered, we will limit our exploration to five of them. First, there is *proxemics*, the study of space and distance. *Kinesics* is the study of bodily movement. *Paralanguage* gives us sounded nonverbal communication, and *haptics* considers touching as a nonverbal variable. Finally, we must confront *chronemics*, that is, how time influences our communication and our perceptions.

In dealing with proxemics, we must include information concerning Albert Meharabian and Edward T. Hall. Meharabian's *immediacy principle* provides a basic nonverbal truth. It says that we get closer to the things and people we like, and we shy away from those that we do not like. Although it can be called a nonverbal truth, it is not a constant. Situational variables may preclude our desire for either distance or closeness.

Edward T. Hall coined the term *proxemics* and provided us with his so-called *spatial zones*. According to Hall, there are four spatial zones. The first is the intimate distance zone. This zone is reserved for your closest friends and family. Your parents, siblings, husband/wife, and/or boyfriend/girlfriend likely fit into this category. The distance between communicators here would most commonly be less than two feet. The second zone is the personal distance zone. This zone includes the people you feel some closeness to but less than the first group—other members of your family, other friends, and/or strong acquaintances. Aunts, uncles, and cousins would be a part of this group, and so would people with whom you have a continuing work relationship. Normally, this communication distance would be less than four feet. The social distance zone is generally less than eight feet and includes weak acquaintances and first meetings with people. The last zone is the public distance zone. It is usually less than twenty-five feet, and it is often the preferred distance from total strangers. Like Mehrabian's immediacy principle, Hall's zones are affected by situational variables.

To fully explore the area of proxemics, we must examine the personal space concept along with some specific variables. Basically, the *personal space* concept says that there is an invisible bubble around each of us. That bubble expands and contracts based on both the need for and the availability of space. The bubble's ability to function may be affected by a series of variables that impact our communication. Let's make a few gross generalizations (usually but not always true) about these variables and how they affect our bubble:

- Personality. The extroverted or outgoing personality type has less need for space than does the introvert. Does this mean that if you meet someone who stays relatively far away from you, you have met an introvert? No. Whatever variables are stronger will determine the bubble size.

- Mood. We tend to require more distance from others when we are in a bad mood than when we are in a good mood.

- Affinity. When we like and trust our communicative partner, we tend to communicate at a closer distance. We increase the distance if we distrust or dislike the person.

- Situation. As David K. Berlo indicates, the situation is the most important variable in the process of communicating. Even if we want to increase the distance between ourselves and someone else, we may not be able to do so due to lack of space. Think of a crowded elevator, for example. At times, we may want to decrease the distance, but existing social conventions make that improper.

- Culture/coculture. For most Americans, three to six feet apart is a comfortable distance for communicating. Persons from some Middle Eastern cultures and some South American cultures communicate comfortably with less than three feet between them. Some Middle Eastern cultures believe that if you cannot feel the other person's breath while talking, you are not at a friendly distance. On the other hand, some Asian cultures require more than six feet for polite and comfortable communication. Even in the United States, there are, for example, regional cocultural differences. Southerners generally communicate at closer distances than do Easterners. While the South and the East claim three-foot and six-foot distances, the West and Midwest communicate at four and five feet. Can you guess which is which?

- Status. The person who is recognized as having the higher status gets to decide the distance for communicating. The ability to increase or decrease that distance is a tool for maintaining authority and status.

- Age. This variable has a bit of a twist to it. Usually, we maintain a close distance to those without our own age group and a farther distance from other age groups. However, children are a major exception. Until taught otherwise, children maintain a close distance to persons of any age group. Sometimes age becomes confused with status. When this is the case, the older person gets to determine the distance for communicating.

- Sex/gender. Although sex/gender is a cocultural variable, it is significant enough to merit its own discussion. As a gross generalization, we note that women maintain a closer distance to one another when communicating than do men; this happens regardless of one's sexual orientation. Why? Seemingly, men are subconsciously programmed to see each other as rivals. The handshake evolved to show that no weapons were being carried. Interestingly, modern men maintain a distance of at least an arm's length when communicating. This is a defensive posture. One male could hold off another male and punch him if it became necessary. Women do not seem to be so programmed to protect themselves from one another, but women do seem inclined to increase the distance between themselves and an unknown male. Here the nonverbal posture is defensive. Men tend to be Sapir-Whorf hypothesis active, and that tendency doesn't always lead to the desired conclusion. The desire to seek intimacy by moving closer may be rebuffed by an equal desire of the other person to protect herself or himself. If a social gathering is filled with both Sapir-Whorf hypothesis active people and Sapir-Whorf passive people, the dance of advance and retreat can readily be observed.

- Race. Like gender, race is a cocultural variable that merits its own discussion. Many have written about how difficult it is to deal with race in America; discussions about it make many persons uncomfortable. Perhaps some of the discomfort comes from the inability to accurately decode what we see. The gross generalization here is that we tend to stand closer to people of the same race and farther away from people of different races. If you work with two people of a different race than yours, you may notice the greater physical closeness when they communicate with each other and the lack of physical closeness when they talk to you. This scenario might be decoded as meaning that they don't like people of your race, but for most persons, this would be a natural tendency.

- Physical size. The size of a person tends to have more impact on males than on females. Again, we must return to the defensive posture. Larger men will let a smaller man approach closer than a man of equal size. The subconscious idea behind this move is that the larger man could take out the smaller man if necessary. On the other hand, a smaller man will generally keep a larger man at a distance for safety's sake.

- Artifact. This variable can easily be manipulated; to understand its impact, go beyond the norm. Artifacts can include such things as how our hair is styled, whether or not cosmetics are worn, and how we accessorize/decorate the body. Spike your hair into a giant green Mohawk and see how close people will let you get to them. If everyone wears his hair that way, you are part of the norm, but when you step outside the norm, it has an impact on conversational distance. Thus, tattoos, body piercings, other types of jewelry, glasses, makeup, and mirrored sunglasses can either put you in the norm or outside the norm. This is always something you should ponder before a job interview. Can you make your norm comparable to the interviewer's norm?

- Dress. A discussion of dress takes us into the realms of color and style. The idea of style is not "stylish" but refers to the three styles of nonverbal dress—casual, professional, and costume. Casual dress is represented by what most students wear to school—a shirt and slacks, a shirt and jeans, a blouse and skirt, a blouse and jeans or slacks. Because casual dress usually fits the norm, it does more to attract people to you than to repel them. Professional dress is more like that found in most offices. For women, it often means a two- or three-piece ensemble (some configuration of skirt, blouse, slacks, dress, and jacket). For men, it includes a shirt and tie, a sports coat and tie, or a suit with the appropriate dressy shirt and slacks. Professional dress seems to command status. Those wearing it are usually allowed to determine the distance for conversation. Costume is atypical dress, and unless you are with like-minded people, it can repel others. The Goth look, the cowboy look, and the motorcycle look are examples of costume-style dress. Color is the other aspect of dress that must be considered. Four colors in particular stand out—blue, gray, red, and black. Sometimes the term *power colors* can be applied. Subconsciously, the wearer of blue may be seen as extremely honest, and the wearer of gray may be seen as sincere. It is no wonder that darker blues and grays are recommended for job interviews. Reds and blacks are helpful to those who already have status/authority. Those colors help to maintain a focus on their power. However, when worn by those without power/authority, they may become subconsciously irritating. Yes, even the colors that we wear can affect the comfortable distance of communication.

The second area of nonverbal behavior is known as *kinesics* and deal with bodily movement of all types. We will consider three kinesic areas—gesticulation, eye contact, and facial expressions. Gesticulation is something that we all do, but not all gestures work the same way. There are three distinctly different types of gesticulation that must be examined.

- *Emblems* are bits of gesticulation that perform the substitution function of nonverbal communication. An emblem is most often used without words to convey a message. "Hello" and "goodbye" waves are examples of emblems. Emblems can accidentally cause problems due to different ways of decoding them. The American emblem for "okay" consists of the thumb and index finger touching, with the other fingers held erect. In Asian countries, this emblem might be decoded as money or zero. In the American Southwest and in the countries of Central and South America, that emblem might be decoded as an obscene gesture. In Tunisia, if you show your teeth while performing such a gesture, you have just announced that you will kill someone.

- *Illustrators* are gestures that must accompany words before they can reasonably be decoded. Telling someone that there are four important points to your message while holding up four fingers is an example of an illustrator. Suppose you walked around with your arm outstretched to a certain height. People might question your sanity, and a good decode might only come if you said, "She was this tall."

- *Adaptors* are fascinating. They are gesticulative habits, they are automatic, they are subconsciously controlled, and they respond easily to situational stress. Self-adaptors manipulate their own bodies. There are nose tweakers, ear tuggers, chin strokers, hand wringers, hair twirlers, and scratchers. Under normal circumstances these behaviors occur at fairly low levels, but, when stress is added, they multiply considerably. A keen observer should be able to easily note the increase. When the average person lies, he or she is under stress, and these behaviors would naturally increase. Does this mean that each time you see significant changes, the other person is lying? No, but it does mean that, for some reason, stress is present. Like self-adaptors, object adaptors react to stress. Object adaptors manipulate objects around them. The male job interviewee who adjusts his tie and eyeglasses repeatedly before the interview is a good example. A former student recounted an employment incident where object adaptors played a major role. One of the local police departments was recruiting 911 operators. Those who got through the first interview were told to report back the next day for a test. When the potential employees arrived, they were all issued a test booklet, a scan sheet, and a #2 pencil. When the signal was given to start, pencils started to break all over the room. People rushed to a pencil sharpener, sharpened their pencils, and went back to the test. The pencils had been designed to malfunction. Some persons were cursing, some were breaking the pencils into two pieces, and some threw them around the room. Those people were excused. If the stress of a breaking pencil sent them over the edge, then they were not the best candidates for 911 operators.

Another major area of kinesics is eye contact. Eye contact is a learned behavior. You likely developed your norm by watching the levels of eye contact used by other members of your family. We can essentially divide Americans into high- and low-eye-contact families. Although different cultures have different rules for eye contact, let's focus on the cocultures in this country. Observers see men as having a higher eye contact level than women. Latinos, Asian Americans, and Native Americans have lower levels of eye contact that white or black Americans. The work of LeFranc and Mayo suggests that black and white Americans use eye contact in virtually opposite ways. Blacks maintain more eye contact while talking and whites while listening. Imagine all the decoding errors that can result from differences in eye contact. Can you provide examples?

The last area of our kinesic discussion concerns facial expressions. Never trust the face. There are over two hundred individual muscles in the face, and we have conscious control of all of them. This means that we can make the face say whatever we want. There are four common ways that we manipulate the face to deceive our communicative partners:

- *Deintensify*. Here we allow only some of what we feel to be seen. If we are sad or angry, the other person will not know to what degree.

- *Overintensify*. This means that we turn in an Academy Award–winning performance and show much more than we feel. Imagine how easy it would be to manipulate someone who accidentally tapped you feelings but led you to turn it into a facial vision of total devastation.

- *Mask*. This means showing the opposite of what you feel. If you are afraid, your face says that you are brave. Masking is described by the adage of "crying on the inside but laughing on the outside."

- *Neutral*. The neutral facial expression means that nothing shows. All of the facial muscles are held in a locked position to avoid giving anything away. Commonly, this is called the *poker face*; a good poker player can sometimes bluff his or her way to a win with so-so cards in hand.

One final consideration of facial expressions involves gender differences. It is estimated that women use 73 to 83 percent more facial expressions than men. Quite a decoding mess could result from gender differences. Who deintensifies best, who masks best, who overintensifies best, and who neutralizes best?

The third form of nonverbal behavior is known as *paralanguage*. Essentially, paralanguage is sounded nonverbal communication and includes vocal characteristics and vocal differentiators. Vocal characteristics help to perform nonverbal communication's regulation function. Pitch, rate, and volume are the major vocal characteristics. *Pitch* is the highness or lowness of the vocal tone. Pitch can change the possible decoding of words. A response in a higher pitch might, for example, indicate that something said was not taken seriously, and a lower-pitched response might indicate the opposite. We change pitch to indicate whether or not something is a question, as well as much more. Like the adaptors, pitch is a stress-affected variable. The pitch of the human voice goes up when a person is under stress. Extremely good listeners can hear subtle changes in pitch. As mentioned before, our rate of speech is determined by the dialectical region in which we live. The rates of speaking are slower in the South and faster on the East Coast. The rate at which we speak can confound the decoding process. For example, a faster rate of speech could indicate excitement or a lack of desire to communicate. If someone talks very slowly and deliberately to you, how intelligent would you think this person considers you to be? Although volume is also stress affected, it takes a large amount of stress to change the volume at which we speak. *Volume* is the loudness or softness of speech. Louder volumes are associated with anger and excitement; softer volumes might be found in more intimate conversations. Usually, it takes the stress of a heated argument to push the volume of the human voice upward without intent, and as long as the argument stays heated, the volume will tend to move to higher levels.

The other aspect of paralanguage is known as *vocal differentiators*. These include special vocalizations or sounds that we make and breakers. *Special vocalizations* are all the unique sounds that humans make. We laugh, we cry, we moan, we groan, and we sigh. Lift an empty box in front of other people, but be sure to moan and groan as you do so. These people will likely assume that you are struggling with a heavy load, and some may even offer to help you with the empty box. If all these sounds were put on a scale with laughter at one end and crying at the other, only the crying behavior would show a gender split. It is estimated to take nine times as much stress to make the average man cry compared to the average woman. However, the same amount of stress will produce laughter or the "nervous giggle" in both men and women. Most special vocalizations communicate what we want them to communicate, but the nervous giggle can cause decoding errors. Can you figure out how this might happen?

Breakers are disfluencies that we use to fill gaps of silence while we think. The most common American English breaking sounds are the *er, uh, ah,* and *um* sounds. Breakers are a natural part of human communication, but they are also the most stress sensitive. Small amounts of stress can cause breakers to double, triple, or quadruple. As stress dissipates, breakers will fall back to their normal levels. Do you think the number of breakers increases when we lie? Could that be detected?

The fourth area of nonverbal behavior is *haptics*, which deals with touch as a communicative variable. A good deal of the time touch communicates intimacy, but how touch communicates it and with whom depends on the type of touch. There are five levels of touching behavior:

- Functional professional touch has little intimacy. It is used to accomplish a particular function. A doctor must touch a patient in order to perform a thorough examination. Cheerleaders must touch one another in order to build pyramids. Functionality, not intimacy, is the key with this form of touching behavior.

- Socially polite touch is often seen in first encounters and is controlled by the prevailing society. The handshake is the standard nonverbal greeting ritual for Americans. Although popular magazines have been claiming that the handshake that turns into a hug is gaining ground as the standard greeting ritual, I think it will take several decades to change if it changes at all.

- Friendship-warmth touch is used to express ongoing interpersonal relationships, as with friends. The most common touching behavior here is the hug. If you are wondering how, despite gender differences, the hug became the most common expression of friendship and warmth, it has to do with numbers. First, around the world, a good number of male friends commonly hug. Second, about 52 percent of the American population is female, and women hug each other as well as men in an expression of friendship. For American men the extended handshake is used to express friendship. You begin with a handshake and with your free hand make a brief second point of contact at the elbow or the shoulder, for example.

- Love-intimacy touch takes a person beyond friendship. Someone who has been hypnotized by Hollywood thinks in terms of kissing behaviors and holding hands, which, by the way, are the second and third most common touching behaviors used to express love and intimacy. The hug is still number 1 here. Then how does one avoid confusion? How do you know if the hug is one of friendship or one of love? Love hugs are longer in duration than friendship hugs. The friendship hug usually involves only upper body contact, while the love hug has full body contact.

- Sexual arousal touch is the most intimate form of touch. There are no most common behaviors, and it is a live-and-learn process. Now would be a good time to discuss the rules and regulations of touching behaviors.

The taboo zones give us the most basic of rules regarding touch. The *taboo zones* are the most off-limits area of the human body. Ordinarily, nobody would venture to touch them except perhaps in the case of sexual arousal or functional professional touch. The first and most off-limits area is the face. The face is the staging area for four of our five senses—sight, sound, smell, and taste. Since those senses are critical to survival, we protect them fiercely. Think about how irritating something as simple as an eye examination can be.

The genital regions are protected to preserve the reproduction of the species. These regions include the genitalia of both sexes as well as the buttocks. A woman's chest is added to this group because, unlike a man's chest, a woman's chest has a reproductive function.

The fourth area is the abdomen. Unlike the heart and lungs, which have a bony structure to protect them, other organs, located in the abdomen, are quite vulnerable. By keeping people away from that region, we lessen the chance for serious injury. The kidneys, spleen, liver, and other abdominal organs benefit from such a move.

The final off-limits area is the thigh. This area is off limits purely because of its proximity to the genital region. An odd hand on the thigh makes the person feel uncomfortable. Although not everyone obeys these rules, and although some people have areas beyond the four that are strictly hands off, the taboo zones give you some understanding of what's behind our touching behaviors.

The last area for nonverbal discussion is *chronemics,* which involves our senses and perceptions of time. There are two major worldviews: monochronic and polychromic. A monochronic worldview sees time as a series of individual events, with one event ending before another begins. Those with a monochronic worldview are not good at multitasking. Those with a polychromic worldview see time as a fully connected spiral ribbon with events flowing into one another. Those with a polychromic worldview are good at multitasking; it seems natural for them to do more than one thing at a time.

From a worldview, we now go to more specific views of time for clock-bound people, natural-bound people, and relational-bound people. Clock-bound people live and die by their clocks and watches. If you ask a clock-bound person about travel (for example, "How far is it to Chicago?"), the answer will be given in terms of hours and/or minutes rather than miles and feet. For this person, clock time is the coin of the land. A natural-bound person has bigger potions of his or her life controlled by nature's clock. Natural-bound people are found mostly in rural areas, where one can experience nature's clock more clearly. There is a preparation season, a planting season, a growing season, and a harvesting season. The natural-bound person has much more energy in the spring and summer, and energy ebbs in the fall and winter. A relational-bound person is very different from the other two. Relational-bound people might normally be clock bound or natural bound, but when a relationship is in crisis, all bets are off. Time seems to lose all meaning, with the person focused myopically on repairing the relationship. To most of us, it would seem silly to be told that the person could not come to school or work because a friend had a problem, but this would make perfect sense to the relational-bound person.

Now that we have gotten our feet wet in the pools of nonverbal communication, we need to move on to a discussion of verbal messages. Because we have studied words so much in our education, we often feel that we can command them at will. However, familiarity in this case does not mean control or even great understanding. Let's begin with what we use the verbal coding system to accomplish. The verbal coding system has three purposes:

- *Labeling* is the function of naming things. If people have the same or similar labels for things, it is much easier to refer to or talk about them. The word *piano* makes referring to a piano much easier than going through a physical description of a piano each time we talk about one.

- *Enhancing emotional interaction* means that we use words to clarify meanings with the middle and lower level emotions. You can tell someone that you love him or hate her by using overt nonverbal cues, but middle and lower emotions might not have such a clear palette to work from. A confused look can be decoded in many different ways, but if you say that you are confused, the message should be better understood.

- The *information exchange* function of verbal communication can often take us back to the Sapir-Whorf hypothesis. Sometimes the word is the thing. If I were to ask you what makes Tuesday "Tuesday" other than the word *Tuesday*, what would you say? If I were to ask you what makes July "July" other than the word *July*, what would you say? Time is an excellent example because time is continuous; it is not naturally segmented into days, months, and years. Our concepts of time are dependent upon the language we speak. Other people living at other times and speaking other languages had a different sense of time.

When considering the verbal coding system, it is better to talk of inherent barriers than behaviors. This indicates that barriers to communicating are a natural part of the language.

The first inherent barrier that we must consider is the barrier of meaning. Linguists tell us that meaning is the understanding that any person has about anything in his or her environment. This appears to be simple; let's play the meaning game to see if it is as simple as it seems. Let's take the word *dog*. I want you to define this word out loud. The only rules to the game are as follows: You cannot use a description because meanings and descriptions are not the same. You cannot use a definition because meanings and definitions are not the same. No descriptions . . . no definitions . . . tell me what the word *dog* means. Although it seems impossible, there is an answer to the question. The word *dog* means the same thing that all the other words of the American English language or of any other language mean. The word, in and of itself, means nothing. Meanings are not inherent in words; meanings are added by source/encoders and receiver/decoders. Still, we throw words at one another and become angry when the way we have encoded a word isn't the way the word is decoded by another person. How could he or she be so stupid?

There are three special word categories, used every day, that often create inherent barriers to communication: relative words, emotive words, and equivocal words:

- *Comparative words* work in communication only if both people have the same standard of comparison. For example, attractive and unattractive must be the same between the two; large and small must be the same as well. If I were to ask how many of you live in small towns, how many of you would immediately raise your hand without first finding out what the standard of comparison was?

- *Value judgment words* are an expression of a person's values but are often confused with valid descriptive words. You can call any car a classic, but calling it that doesn't make it one. You might call the car a classic due to positive memories associated with the car, like the birth of your daughter in the backseat. However, would that enhance the value of the car to a buyer? If someone calls what you are wearing *tacky*, it means that he or she doesn't like it. It doesn't necessarily mean that there is something wrong with the clothing or with you for buying it. People get beat up when they confuse someone's opinion with a true description. A true description is consistent and won't usually generate an argument. An emotive word is a value judgment that is changeable and can generate an argument. Saying that the sweater is red is a description. Saying that the sweater is fashionable is a value judgment.

- A *changeable word* deals with intangible things; there isn't always a clear physical construct for changeable words. Changeable words have multiple diverse meanings as well. *Love* is the most changeable word in the American English language. Do you really know what someone means when he or she declares his or her love for you? Let's pose a philosophical question. If a store clerk gives you too much change, what would be the honest thing to do? What would you do in the case of the changeable word *honesty*?

Allegedly, American English is the most difficult language for a nonnative to learn to speak competently. Our language is so difficult because there are so many code variations. In fact, linguists argue that even native-born speakers will not likely master all the variations within their lifetime. When I think of code variations, I immediately think of slang. There is no goodness or badness, no rightness or wrongness, to slang. All slang is a group vocabulary difference. There is work-related slang, age group–related slang, regional slang, activity-based slang, religious slang, and neighborhood slang. Doctors have doctor slang to communicate with other doctors. Lawyers have lawyer slang, and mechanics have mechanic slang. In the South, whence I hail, the regional slang means that all soft drinks are called *cokes* or *pops* or (very rural) *dopes*. If you order a coke, you will be asked what kind of coke you want. You can get a coke-coke or a Pepsi-coke or an orange-coke or a grape-coke.

Another major code variation is that of euphemisms. We use euphemisms as polite substitutes to avoid making people feel uncomfortable about the topic at hand. We have euphemisms that make death seem nicer, and we have euphemisms that make sex sound more pristine. If you ever need to amuse yourself, think of all the terms we have coined for urinating and defecating.

Finally, the way a word sounds is a code variation and can lead to a communication breakdown in some situations. You speak with an accent whenever you are speaking a language for which you do not naturally have phonetic habits. A *phonetic habit* is the physical method of sound production, and each language has its own. Since prior to the age of twelve the only language that I learned was American English. I can imitate the rolling *r* of Spanish languages or imitate the low guttural sounds of the Germanic languages. However, I can produce none of those sounds exactly as a native-born speaker would. I produce the sounds of the American English language with a dialect. A *dialect* is a regional variation in terms of rate/resonation, grammar, and vocabulary. Though I produce the sounds like any other American English speaker, my preferred resonating chambers and the rate make the sounds come out differently. For example, people in Wisconsin resonate more in the nasal passages, people in Tennessee resonate more in the throat, people in Illinois resonate more in the mouth, and people in Alabama resonate more in the chest cavity. When you add different rates of speech to the mix, a sound that was physically produced the same way comes out sounding very different.

Perhaps the biggest stumbling block of all comes from how we use the verbal coding system. Even if we could eliminate all the other inherent barriers, our use of the verbal coding system would likely still lead to communication breakdowns. There are a few verbal code usage problems that merit discussion:

- Conclusion jumping. When we jump to a conclusion without a solid basis for doing so, we have inferred. For example, imagine that you have been watching a preschool class. You see one little boy who doesn't follow instructions. Often, the teacher has to take objects from him so that he will move on to the next project. Is the child ill-mannered? Is he a brat? Is he hard of hearing? All are viable explanations for the behavior you have witnessed, and you would likely jump to one conclusion over the others. But there is no basis in fact for the inferential leap.

- Valence words. *Valence words* have either a positive or a negative charge. They are used to produce a reaction in the listener. The Sapir-Whorf hypothesis tells us that sometimes communicators use valence words in order to produce a desired response from the listener. A politician, for example, might want a conservative audience to reject the ideas of his opponent. Thus, the politician will spend his speech referring to his opponent's ideas as *liberal*. Whether the ideas are liberal or not doesn't matter; the purpose of using the word *liberal* is to evoke that negative response. People will often react more strongly to the word than to the thing it represents. Valence words apply to situations as well as to people and ideas. Tell a group of college students that their next test will be very, very difficult. When the test is given, students will miss test questions because they are looking for trick questions. If the professor said that the test was hard, then none of the questions can be that easy to answer. The students are trapped by valence words.

- The know-it-all may spend a lot of time tasting shoe leather. This kind of person thinks that he or she knows all there is to know about something. This person also thinks that what he or she knows is all there is to know. If we apply this attitude to a communicative situation, the know-it-all believes that he or she can account for all the variables in the communication situation. If you have ever stuck your foot in your mouth, it was likely due to your know-it-all attitude.

- Locked communication is a denial of growth and change in people. We developed communication strategies to deal with people, and we want them to stay the same. Parents often have this trouble when children grow to adulthood. Although it might be easier to continue the adult/child relationship, a new way of relating to the offspring is important for effective communication. An entire society can penalize a group due to frozen evaluations. For example, for a long time, our society through of women as passive, fragile, weak-minded, emotional, and immature. As long as that was the prevailing view, there were not many female truck drivers or surgeons. As long as the words kept the communication locked, there wasn't much progress for women. However, as the communication strategies were unlocked, we discovered the myriad things that women could do.

- The extreme split is the last stop on our verbal code usage cavalcade. *Polarization* means the creation of false dichotomies—the need to see everything as black or white, as right or wrong, or as good or bad. These false dichotomies are apt to generate a breakdown in the communication process unless the two communicators have the same polarized views. Extreme split people probably are not born that way, but they become that way over a period of time. The more extreme split terms a person uses, the more polarized that person's thinking becomes. It becomes like a snowball effect, with polarized thought feeding into polarized words and polarized words feeding into extreme split thought.

As you can see, in language, both words and nonwords are interesting and complex. Developing a fuller understanding of both sides of language can help improve our ability to communicate with others.

Romaine, Suzanne. *Language in Society. Oxford: Oxford University Press, 1994.*

Swoyer, Chris. *Stanford Encyclopedia of Philosophy, Stanford: Stanford University Press, 2003.*

Meharabian, Albert. *Silent Messages. Wadsworth: Belmont, California, 1971.*

Meharabian, Albert. *Nonverbal Communication. Aldine-Atherton: Chicago, Illinois, 1972.*

Hall, Edward. *The Silent Language. Garden City, N.Y.: Doubleday, 1959.*

Hall, Edward. *The Hidden Dimension. Garden City, N. U. :Doubleday, 1966.*

Berlo, David. *The Process of Communication. New York: Holt, Rhinehart, and Winston, 1960.*

Communication Situations: Cultures and Cocultures

The study of intercultural communication is only a few decades old, and it had a very rocky beginning. Intercultural communication technically should be considered a comparison of communication from different cultures. However, some argue differently and state that intercultural communication has existed under many names. It has been called *cross-cultural communication, trans-racial communication*, and *diverse communication*, as well as many other names. Technically, a comparison of communication within one culture but from different cocultures should be called *intracultural communication*. However, in the last decade, *intercultural communication* became the most widely accepted name for this area of communication study involving both cultures and cocultures.

In the early days of this field of study, people were dissuaded from focusing on intercultural communication. It was considered trendy, it was labeled as unimportant, and it was deemed an inferior area of academic study. The attitudes of the past seem quite ironic when you consider the importance of this area today. Most major universities and colleges see the study of intercultural communication as an anchor to the entire study of communication. In fact, many universities are beginning to require the course as a part of meeting general education standards. During the last decade, the growth of programs, classes, and majors in the area of intercultural communication has been phenomenal.

So, what is intercultural communication? For our purposes, intercultural communication is defined as **the study of the impacts that cultural and cocultural differences have on communication encoding and decoding. It is designed to help the student develop a better understanding of communication differences (both verbal and nonverbal) and strategies that will improve his or her communication with diverse groups of people**.

Within this framework, the terms *culture* and *coculture* take on special significance. Thus, the next logical step should be to explain these terms. The average person who hears the term *culture* is likely to think in terms of music, art, dance, or architecture. Those things are a part of we call *objective culture*. However, our concern with objective culture will be mostly peripheral. Intercultural communication is mainly concerned with *subjective culture*. As a result, we will use the term *culture* to mean the attitudes, beliefs, values, and behaviors common to people within a particular country or a particular region including multiple countries. As an example, we can say that there is a U.S. culture and that there is a North American culture.

The other critical term for us to understand is *coculture*, which refers to a group of people who have attitudes, beliefs, values, and behaviors different from those of other groups within a particular culture. Cocultures can be based on gender, race, socioeconomic status, religion, physical ability, population density, physical size, geographic location, age, and many other characteristics. Though you may be the product of one culture, you are the product of many cocultures. Not all of your cocultures will have the same impact upon your communication or interaction with others. A difficult but important thing for you to know is which of your cocultures have the greatest impact on how you communicate and interact with others.

You may now be wondering why cultures and cocultures are important to communication. A person's culture and cocultures essentially determine perceptions. How messages are encoded, transferred, and decoded are all heavily reliant on cultures and cocultures. The impact that culture and cocultures have on communication is both habitual and subconsciously oriented. Men, for example, would not receive a message from another person and consciously think that because they are males, the message must be interpreted in a particular way. Yet, subconsciously, that is exactly what happens; the process is subtle and automatic. *In part, the study of intercultural communication makes communicators more consciously aware of the cultural and cocultural variables that affect the encoding, transmission, and decoding of our own communication as well as the communication of others.*

The attitudes, beliefs, values, and behaviors that come from our culture and our cocultures are passed along to us both intentionally and unintentionally. We absorb them from our families, our neighborhoods, our schools, our churches, and many other sources. It could be said that they hard-wire the brain with specific programming. Once set, these habits become automatic, and without the interference of the conscious mind, they will continue.

How often do you wonder whether or not you should wear clothes when you leave your home? The likely answer is, never. One facet of American culture is the wearing of clothes in public places. No conscious thought is required to make that decision each day; we simply follow our cultural pattern. Likewise, there are cocultural patterns that drive our decisions, but those patterns may differ from one cocultural group to another.

There are great benefits to our overall communication skills when we are able to recognize these cultural and cocultural patterns both in ourselves and in the people with whom we communicate.

Before moving on, we must also examine the encoding and decoding processes of communication. *Encoding* refers to the act of preparing a message to be transmitted to another person. When we we want to communicate with another person, our minds formulate a clear picture of our thoughts. However, we cannot send these thoughts to the other person. Instead, we have to encode them into verbal and nonverbal symbols that can be transmitted. Even when common languages are spoken, different cultures will encode messages differently because of the cultural hard wiring of the brain. Although Americans, when communicating with each other, may encode in similar ways, cocultural influences may cause differing encoding processes to occur. As an example, men and women may encode the same message very differently. *Decoding* refers to the process of receiving verbal and nonverbal symbols and converting them into a picture or word picture in the brain. Again, different cultures using a common language may achieve very different results. Cocultural differences can also cause the decoding results to be very different.

Cultures, cocultures, encoding, and decoding are some of the major variables that a competent and effective intercultural communicator must understand. As a communicator gains knowledge of intercultural communication, he or she should also be able to improve overall communication skills and should be able to communicate with diverse groups of people with greater comfort.

It will be helpful to engage in a couple of exercises. The first one is an exercise relating to cocultures. Try to identify at least ten of your cocultures. Also, attempt to rank order them in terms of how important each one is in affecting your communication and interaction with others. Following are some of my cocultures; you can use the form below to list your own. In addition, try to provide a rationale for your ranking.

Coculture Exercise (Things to Ponder)

Professor's Example:

1. Communication professional

2. Male

3. African American

4. Middle class

5. East Tennessean

6. Rural

7. Physically able

8. Christian

9. Family member

10. Pet owner

Student's Example

COCULTURE   RANK

_____   _____

_____   _____

_____   _____

_____   _____

_____   _____

_____   _____

_____   _____

_____   _____

_____   _____

_____   _____

We are all citizens of the Milky Way galaxy, and we are all members of planet Earth. However, these truths do not define our umbrella cultural identity. Why? It is a bit difficult to explain beyond indicating the role of habit in our lives. As children, we were taught that we were members of particular cultures (also known as *umbrella cultures*), and that idea likely prevailed. Those of us who grew up in the United States do not call ourselves North Americans after the region in which we live. We do not feel as strong an allegiance to Canada or Mexico as we do to our own country. Situation (location) and history (length of habit) seem to be the major determinants of our cultural/umbrella cultural identities. Yet, these factors do not seem to be the most important ones determining our cocultural identities. This leads to an interesting question: Where exactly do our cocultural identities come from? Let's explore some of the possibilities.

There are four prime theories of cocultural identity development, and students of intercultural communication should become familiar with each of them. Since situation and history have the greatest impact on the formation of cultural identities, we will focus on the development of cocultural identities.

First, the work of Martin and Nakayama brings us the *avowal/ascription theory of cocultural identity development*. This theory deals with the impacts that internal and external forces have on the development of our cocultural identities. The external forces are represented by *ascription*. If these forces are stronger, they will determine our cocultural identity. The internal forces are represented by *avowal*. If these forces are stronger, they will control the development of our cocultural identity.

As an example, consider the fact that some of my students might decide that I am old because I have lived for half a century (*ascription*). However, I consider myself to be young (*avowal*). The collision of these two forces will produce a champion. If the outside forces are stronger, they will determine how I perceive myself. If the internal forces are stronger, they will control my self-perception.

Sometimes, avowal/ascription can be the source of intercultural conflict. When the outside forces, for example, choose and interact with only one aspect of a person's cocultures, this is called *discounting communication*. Discounting communication is any form of verbal or nonverbal communication that ignores or diminishes another person's sense of competence, autonomy, or identity. Let's imagine for a moment that I decided to choose the coculture you ranked as ninth on your cocultural identity list. I will only relate to you in that sense. The rest of what you perceive yourself to be is ignored. Unless you do not have an integrated sense of self or a strong sense of avowal, my actions would likely cause conflict between us.

Nonetheless, the stronger of the two (avowal and ascription) will determine a person's cocultural identity. This, by the way, can vary from situation to situation. An adult may have a strong sense of competence and autonomy at work due to his or her avowal, but when that adult visits his or her parents, ascription may evoke more childlike responses, thoughts, and feelings. Thus, we can conclude that avowal/ascription help to form situational identities as well as an overall sense of self.

Second, empowered cocultures, says Rita Hardiman, form their identities slightly differently from nonempowered cocultures. Before we consider Hardiman's *theory of empowered cocultural identity development*, the terms *empowered* and *nonempowered* need to be analyzed. An *empowered coculture* is a coculture that has a long history of operating mostly freely and generally is unencumbered by the perceptions and actions of other cocultures. Males, whites, the educated, the upper class, and the middle class are examples of empowered cocultures. A *nonempowered coculture*, by contrast, has a long history of being unable to operate freely and generally is encumbered by the perceptions and actions of other cocultures. The working class, Latinos, women, African Americans, and the undereducated are examples of traditionally nonempowered cocultures. However, once again, the variable of situation has to be considered. Some situations will rob the traditionally empowered, and some situations will change the role of the traditionally nonempowered.

Now, let us get back to the work of Rita Hardiman. Hardiman believes that there are five stages in the formation of identity for empowered cocultures. It is important to note that fully cycling through the stages is not always what happens. Members of some cocultures never fully cycle through; they may remain in one stage throughout their lives. It should also be noted that those who do cycle through will take varying periods of time to do so.

Hardiman's first stage is called *unexamined identity*. At this stage, there is no fear of those who exhibit different characteristics, and there is no sense of superiority to those who are different. At stage two, called *acceptance*, the worldview that others are inferior, or are broken and need help, is adopted. This worldview can be embraced either consciously or subconsciously. When stage three (*resistance*) is reached, other cocultures are not seen as bad, but the problems that exist are blamed on the person's particular empowered coculture. In *redefinition*, the fourth stage, there is no longer self-blame for the problems that exist. The final stage is *integration*. When this stage is reached, the person begins to incorporate all of his or her cocultures into a cohesive whole. At this stage, the person is much more likely to be able to perceive, accept, and respect differences in others. He or she is also more likely to operate by evaluating on a case-by-case basis rather than using excessive generalizations.

As an example, let's generalize a bit with the male gender. When we men are very young, we generally do not recognize gender differences (*unexamined identity*), but we eventually do reach a level of perception where gender differences are noted. Often, we will brand the other gender as less valuable than our own. We may consider women less strong and less physically competitive. We may even objectify them (*acceptance*). Some men, but not necessarily all, may move to a point where great empathy and sympathy are expressed for the plight of women in our society. As men, we may feel a sense of responsibility for the existing situation (*resistance*). If a man progresses, he will get to a point where the sense of guilt is not a motivator. The problem is still recognized, but his personal sense of being fully responsible for the problem is gone (*redefinition*). Assuming that the man is moving forward in the development of his identity, he will begin to reduce the myopic nature of his maleness. He will embrace his other cocultures and recognize their importance in terms of his full sense of self (*integration*).

The *theory of nonempowered cocultural identity development* is based on the work of Ponterotto and Pederson and indicates that there are four stages. Again, note that not everyone will cycle through all the stages, some will get stuck in one stage, and varying amounts of time will be required for those who cycle through all the stages. As in Hardiman's theory, the first stage is called *unexamined identity*. There is no recognition of differences here, and the cocultural identity remains unexplored. In the *conformity* stage, the values, beliefs, attitudes, and behaviors of the most relevant empowered coculture will be internalized rather than those of the person's own coculture. Generally and eventually for some people, some form of dissonance will trigger the *resistance and separation* stage. At this stage, everything save the person's particular coculture will be abandoned, and the person will become immersed in his or her own coculture. The fourth and final stage is called *integration*. In this stage, the person develops a sense of self-respect as well as respect for the cocultures of others. Once again, all of the person's cocultures are unified into a cohesive whole.

Here, let's generalize using Native Americans as our example. In early life, a Native American child might not recognize all of the surrounding cocultural differences. There may be no desire to explore the child's own coculture (*unexamined identity*). If those who are perceived as successful are different, there could be a tendency to imitate them as a way of likewise achieving success (*conformity*). Suppose that, at some point, those being imitated or others choose to highlight the Native American's differences in some discounting way. Enough dissonance may be produced by the discounting to cause rejection of the imitation and total immersion in the Native American coculture. This immersion would exclude the racial cocultures of others and would diminish the value of the Native American's other cocultures (*resistance and separation*). Some, but not necessarily all, may move to a point where being Native American is part but not all of who the person is. His or her other cocultures are embraced and valued as well (*integration*).

Tina Harris tells us that developing one's cocultural identity is an ongoing process. The *theory of definition/redefinition cocultural identity development* says that we negotiate the elements of our cocultural identity with others. That identity will be *formed, maintained, and modified* as necessary. Harris indicates that our cocultural identity is not just in flux due to situational variables, but that individual communicative relationships require regular adaptation of the cocultural identity as well. As an example, think of how friendships you have had over the years have changed. If we exclude situational variables, chances are good that those people who continued the negotiating process and allowed you to modify your identity with them as needed are still your friends. By contrast, those who did not continue to negotiate and who wanted to lock you into a particular identity probably are not still close to you.

The development of our cocultural identities is a complex set of processes. Knowing how some of these processes work is critical in attempting to understand and communicate successfully with those who are like us as well as those who are not.

Things to Ponder

Take a second look at your cocultural list as well as the other lists that have been posted. Ponder the following and list your responses:

- Did ascription or avowal put the most cocultures on your list?

- Are the top five cocultures on your list dominated by empowered or nonempowered cocultures?

- Was the rank ordering the result of a negotiated process?

- Would the rank ordering be the same if the list was executed in a different situation (at home versus at work, for example)?

- Based on the other cocultural lists, with whom do you think you could develop the strongest friendship? (*My hypothesis of affinity suggests that when a majority of the items in the top five slots of the coculture list are the same for two people and are given similar weight by both of them, there is a strong potential for a viable interpersonal relationship.*)

From an intercultural standpoint, there are two primary states of existence. The first state is called *ethnocentric*. This state is characterized by a belief in the normalcy or rightness of only one's own culture and/or one's own cocultures. Further, all evaluation (consciously or subconsciously) of people, events, and things uses one's own culture and/ or cocultures as the standard or benchmark. There are varying degrees of ethnocentrism and, thus, different ethnocentric stages.

The second state is called *ethnorelative*. In this state, the tendency is to be more accepting of differences and to evaluate people, events, and things with appropriate standards or benchmarks. As in the ethnocentric state, there are degrees of ethnorelativism and, thus, multiple stages.

Ethnocentrism is a very natural human tendency, whereas ethnorelativism is more of a learned behavior. Sometimes, but not always, life experiences or education might help a person move from communicating predominantly from the ethnocentric state to communicating primarily from the ethnorelative state. Some people, however, never get beyond the ethnocentric stages, and it is not rare for someone who operates mostly from the ethnorelative stages to revert to some ethnocentric behaviors and modes of communication.

If a person's life experiences do not involve regular or significant encounters with those from different cultures/cocultures, ethnorelativism is not enhanced. If educational experiences do not include courses like this one or courses with elements of diversity education, little may be done to help a person move to ethnorelative stages.

In the 1990s, Dr. Milton J. Bennett devised what he called a *developmental model of intercultural sensitivity.* Though Bennett's model was originally only intended to deal with differing cultures, it has been adapted to apply to differing cocultures as well. Let us examine Bennett's model and its implications for improving intercultural understanding and self-awareness.

Bennett indicated that there were three stages of ethnocentrism: denial, defense, and minimization. Let's explore each of them.

At the *denial* stage, there is usually an inability to fully construe cultural or cocultural differences. A person in this ethnocentric stage would likely engage in benign stereotyping and/or making only superficial statements of tolerance. Consciously or subconsciously, there is a tendency to dehumanize those who are significantly different.

Sometimes denial is the result of natural isolation. If a person is only exposed to his or her own homogeneous group, the opportunity, as well as the motivation, to construct relevant categories for noticing and interpreting cultural and cocultural differences will not exist. At other times, denial is the result of intentional separatism. Intentionally isolating oneself from significant cultural or cocultural differences protects one's own cultural and cocultural views of the world.

At the denial stage, a person can be superficially benign toward differences; aggressively ignorant because he or she believes there is no need to comprehend differences; or exploitive of differences.

The second ethnocentric stage is called *defense.* This stage is characterized by an "us/them" mentality. A person at this stage recognizes cultural and cocultural differences but has a negative evaluation of them. In fact, the greater the difference, the more negative the evaluation will be. The negative evaluation can take one of two forms: either overt denigration of cultural/cocultural differences or exaggeration of the positive aspects of one's own culture/cocultures compared to others.

At the defense stage, a person has better-elaborated but poorly integrated cultural/cocultural categories; has a siege mentality in which privilege and/or identity are highly protected; engages in intentional seclusion from those who are different, and may overtly or covertly support negative actions toward those who are different; and has no support for the concept of equal opportunity.

The final ethnocentric stage is called *minimization.* The duality of this stage allows for the recognition of superficial cultural differences, but it maintains that basically all people are exactly the same. The emphasis at this stage is on the similarity of people and the commonality of values. However, the ideas of similarity and commonality are couched in the ethnocentric idea that those who are "different" are really like us. One's own culture/cocultures are still the benchmark.

One phase of minimization is called *physical universalism,* and the minimization is accomplished by relying on the commonality of the related physical aspects of being human. The other phase of minimization is called *transcendent universalism.* This phase claims commonality based solely on subordination to particular religious or social philosophies.

Though the behavior of people at the minimization stage is extremely nice, they still ignore the differences of others. Also, ironically, they enjoy institutionalized privileges but deny that they even exist.

Most, but not all, people will move beyond the ethnocentric stages. Life experiences and/or specific educational experiences will provide the motivation to move on to the ethnorelative stages. The timetable for this move has myriad possibilities. Some will make the transition when they are relatively young, some will not make the transition until their middle years, and some will make it only in their later years. Though often viewed as more positive, the ethnorelative stages present in one of the stages a virtually unreachable goal. Let's examine the three stages of ethnorelativism: acceptance, adaptation, and integration.

The first ethnorelative stage is *acceptance.* With this stage comes the recognition and appreciation of cultural/cocultural differences. Acceptance marks the beginning of a person's ability to interpret events/phenomena contextually. Acceptance manifests itself at two different levels. The first level is called *behavioral relativism*, and a person at this level knows that behaviors exist within a cultural context and must be analyzed within that context. *Value relativism,* the second level, causes a person to understand that beliefs and values exist within a cultural context and leads the person away from absolutism and value/belief polarization.

At the acceptance stage, people are motivated to learn about various cultures/cocultures, including their own. They have curiosity without fear.

Adaptation is the second ethnorelative stage. It is here that the best foundation for communication skills that work across cultures and cocultures is laid. Adaptation has two major characteristics. *Empathy*, the first characteristic, means that a person has the conscious ability to shift perspectives and act in culturally/coculturally appropriate ways. *Pluralism,* the other characteristic, means that a person has internalized other cultural/cocultural views and can shift behavioral frames without much conscious effort.

Although adaptation is not the final ethnorelative stage, it is most likely the final stage that people will be able to reach. Although Bennett's model includes a third ethnorelative stage, that stage is more theoretical than practical. Let us now consider it.

Integration is the final ethnorelative stage. At this stage, a person would maintain only a marginal identity of his or her own and would be able to shift readily into and out of various cultural/cocultural identities. The person, if he or she existed, would be a cultural/cocultural chameleon and likely would exist only on the fringes of good mental health.

Bennett's model provides a good framework in which to operate. It should be noted that communication can be functional within the ethnocentric stages, but the likelihood of communication breakdowns due to encoding and decoding errors is high. Within the first two ethnorelative stages, communication moves more from functional to effective. Fewer communication breakdowns occur, and, though still not exact, encoding and decoding are handled more from a cultural/cocultural contextual standpoint. If it were possible for a person to abandon any sense of personal cultural/cocultural identities and adopt those of the communication partner, communication would be enhanced, but perhaps at the expense of good mental health.

Things to Ponder

- Using Bennett's developmental model, where would you say you are currently? Why?

- Without using names, can you provide an example(s) of denial from people with whom you have interacted?

- Without using names, can you provide an example(s) of defense from people with whom you have interacted?

- Without using names, can you provide an example(s) of minimization from people with whom you have interacted?

- Without using names, can you provide an example(s) of acceptance from people with whom you have interacted?

- Without using names, can you provide an example(s) of adaptation from people with whom you have interacted?

- Combining what you learned in the second online lecture with this lecture, speculate on why integration would not be in one's best interest.

Martin, Judith and Thomas Nakayama. *Intercultural Communication in Contexts. McGraw-Hill, 2003.*

Brown, Tom. *Understanding and A[[;uing of Racial Identity Theory: Rita Hardiman's. White Identity Developoment: a Stage Model. Rochester Institute of Technology, 2008.*

Ponterotto, J and Pedersen, J. Preventing Prejudice. *Newbury Park, Ca.: Sage, 1993.*

Harris, Tina and Orbe, Mark. *Interracial Communication. Sage Publications, 2007.*

Bennett, Milton J. *(ed.) Basic Concepts of Intercultural Communication. Yarmouth, Me. Intercultural Press, 1998.*

Communication Situations: Small Groups and Interpersonal Conflict

The ability to work well with others is a highly prized skill desired by employers, but often, working in groups is something many people strongly dislike. The irony is that what cements a good interpersonal relationship is what we are most leery of in a group situation. Interdependence is the cornerstone of both a good interpersonal relationship and a successful group working relationship.

Let's begin by asking ourselves how a small group is defined. One criterion would be size. Let's say that a small group can range from three to around fifteen people. Two people are a dyad rather than a small group. Three people mark the initial development of communicative subunits. A *communicative subunit* is a smaller group in which communication flows more freely than within the entire group. Of course, member interdependence must also be present in any successful small group. A workable small group should have goals. Sometimes, the goals are terminal; the group disbands once they are reached. Sometimes, the goals are ongoing; the group keeps functioning even though its membership may undergo significant changes.

A group may be defined by its structure. If we took a collection of people with no significant common ties, no established lines of communication, no common goal, and no chain of command, we would have what is called a *pedestrian group*. More accurately, since it is not a true group, we could call it a *grouping*. If we took the same collection of people and gave them a common goal, such as moving a piano, they would be a *selected group*. If the same people with the common goal were given time to establish effective lines of communication, we would call them a *concerted group*. And finally, if we took a group of people with effective lines of communication and a common goal and helped them develop a chain of command, we would have an *organized group*.

A group can also be defined by its function. There are both social groups and task-oriented groups. *Social groups* often help people fulfill their interpersonal need to be with and communicate with other people. *Task-oriented groups* are given the jobs of information gathering, information disseminating, and/or problem solving.

If there is enough time and lack of substantial external pressure, groups go through a five-stage process of formation:

- The *forming* stage is the most tentative. During this stage, group members analyze one another or size each other up. This is the "play nice" stage, and often only the best foot is put forward. Though each prson is seeking a sphere of influence, subtlety is the mode of operation. This stage cannot last forever if the group hopes to reach a workable, viable level.

- The *storming* stage, for most groups, is very uncomfortable. Who the members really are and what they really want tends to shine through. It is often like an adult version of "King of the Hill." Storming is a necessary stage in group development; it helps group members see what needs to be done to have a good working relationship.

- The *norming* stage is the effort to get past all the bumps in the road. After storming, group members can clearly see the need to develop a code of conduct, a chain of command, and rules of operation. Without the storming stage, the norming stage would resemble lemmings following each other off a cliff.

- The *performing* stage occurs after modes of operation are determined. The process of refining working relationships is the order of business. Once at this stage, a group can move toward accomplishing its goals.

- The *reforming* stage is subject to circumstances. To reform means to recycle through all the stages once more but in an abbreviated form. Changes in membership and external pressure or changes in deadlines can precipitate the reforming stage.

There are various group theories as well. Let's begin with the *rules theory*. This theory doesn't believe in interpersonal relationships without boundaries; instead, it states that groups should formalize those boundaries by creating rules. A rule is a pattern that can be followed. A rule should be prescriptive to particular situations or behaviors that are not desired. It should establish a penalty or consequence for ignoring the boundaries. Overall, the purpose of rules is to help a group establish its own norms. On the other hand, the rules theory suggests that it would be a serious error to try to develop rules that tell people how to think or feel.

The *social exchange theory* can tell you a good deal about the consequences of group membership. If the costs (in terms of time, money, or other resources) of belonging to a group are greater than the rewards, the group is likely to falter. At the very least, social loafing—goofing off without seriously contributing to the functions of the group—will increase. If the rewards of belonging to a group (friendships, communication partners) are greater than the costs, the group will likely remain viable.

Since we are examining groups, this is also a good place to examine interpersonal conflict, which is found in both group and interpersonal relationships. Let's begin with some myths about conflict. The first myth is that for the good of the group or the good of the interpersonal relationship, conflict should be avoided at all costs. If this were true, it might often mean that you could not express what you thought or felt. Communicating is more than just the exchange of facts; it also involves opinions and feelings. The second myth is that conflict is due only to a lack of understanding between friends or group members. In fact, two people or a group of people can understand one another's positions and still disagree. The final myth is that all conflicts can be resolved. Some conflict runs as deep as who we are, and unless we are willing to abandon our identities, that kind of conflict will remain as a barrier to some group members and some friends. It just cannot be resolved.

There are truths about conflict, and one of the hardest truths to accept is that conflict is necessary. Conflict is a natural part of human growth and development; without it we might stagnate. Second, conflict comes from communicating with others. If we never heard a difference of opinion, a difference in feeling, and/or a different point of view, we could avoid conflict. An additional truth is that conflict is affected by our style of communication, which can control conflict depth and generate conflict longevity. Fourth and finally, though not all conflicts can be resolved, most of them can be managed. We can set aside the conflict triggers for the good of an interpersonal relationship or a group relationship.

Understanding the different types of conflict is important to maintaining a good interpersonal relationship or a good group working relationship. When conflict occurs, the first thing you need to do is to pull back on the emotional throttle. Having a conflict without emotional restrictions is simply inviting disaster. If you are involved in a serious interpersonal conflict, stop and ask yourself if all the shared memories and feelings are something that you really want to sacrifice. If you are involved in a serious group conflict, stop and ask yourself if the consequences of not reaching the group's goal are worth the sacrifice. Often, these two steps provide a modicum of emotional control and make handling the conflict easier. Let's look at the different types of conflict:

- *Affective conflict* is based on injured feelings. Something was said or done by one party that hurts the feelings of another party. Affective conflicts are most often accidental. The best thing to do is to offer a sincere apology for the hurt feelings and assure the person that it was not an intentional act. Affective conflicts are usually resolvable.

- *Substantive conflict* is fact or information based. This conflict is really a question of who is right and who is wrong. Strange as it may seem, substantive conflicts can get intense. To resolve this sort of conflict, find an acceptable, qualified source that can provide a definitive answer.

- *Normative conflict* deals with behavioral expectations. We all have expectations as to how our friends and/or group members should behave. When those expectations are violated, the result is normative conflict. Since we cannot control the behavior of others, normative conflict is not always resolvable. Sometimes, it has to be managed. Perhaps you and the other person can reach an agreement that the behavior will not be exhibited in your presence.

- *Value conflict* stems from differing belief systems. When people have opposing beliefs about what is right/wrong and/or good/bad, value conflict is not far away. Because our values are so strongly tied to our identities, value conflict is not resolvable. You would have to be willing to abandon your entire belief system and adopt another one to resolve it. At best, value conflict can be managed. This may require, for example, the avoidance of certain topics of discussion, but management is possible.

© Ed Kashi/Corbis

- *Ego-based conflict* has one goal: to win. This conflict deals with opinions and comparisons. Unlike substantive conflict, there are no definitive answers here, only other opinions. Questions like "Who was the best boxer of all times?" or "Who was the most talented Miss America ever?" can be argued endlessly. Luckily, ego-based conflict rarely becomes intense, but when it does, it can be managed. It can't be resolved, but it can be set aside or time limited as a topic of conversation. Here, you have to just agree to disagree.

Courtesy of the Miss America Organization

Though it may seem a bit dramatic, you always must remember that what you say in the heat of conflict can affect the survival of an interpersonal or a working group relationship. Always think before you speak!

Communication Situations: The Speaker and Audience Deconstructed

There are two types of analyses that a speaker needs to conduct prior to a public speech. First, there is *self-analysis*. The purpose of self-analysis is to help the speaker determine what kind of speaker he or she is. Understanding personal strengths and weaknesses means that speakers can compensate for their weaknesses and play to their strengths.

Self-analysis revolves around understanding speaker styles, which are usually culturally driven. In the United States, we can associate speaker styles with various cocultures. However, these associations are based on gross generalizations. In communication, a gross generalization represents something that communication studies have shown to be generally but not always the case. Gross generalizations represent likelihoods, not truisms. In addition, gross generalizations don't always express the degree to which a group is subject to the likelihood. Differences in degree are often very important to consider.

There are six *communication styles* that should be considered. The first style is called the *linear speaker style*. In this style, the communication moves in a straight line (from specific to general) and develops explicitly stated connections among subpoints to support an endpoint. Is this your style of communicating? The strength of this style is that it appears logical, and listeners who use a similar style would find it easy to follow. Some cocultures that often employ this style include men, the educated, and those higher on the socioeconomic ladder. The weakness is that most audiences are not composed of persons who regularly employ this style. Those audiences may find it harder to follow or simply less interesting.

Second, there is the *circular speaker style*. The discourse is conducted in a circular movement (from general to specific) by developing context around the main point. That main point is often more subtlely stated; the use of stories and other narratives is characteristic of this style. Are you a circular-style speaker? Those who don't employ this style may find it hard to follow and may even tend to call it disorganized. However, few would call it uninteresting. Women, African Americans, Latino Americans, Asian Americans, Native Americans, those who are moderately educated, and those not at the upper end of the socioeconomic scale are examples of cocultures that generally tend to use this style.

The third speaker style is the *attached speaker style.* This style deals with delivery as opposed to structure, as the linear and circular styles do. A speaker employing the attached style discusses issues with feeling and emotion; this conveys the speaker's stake in the outcome of the situation. Though this style is generally quite compelling, some listeners could end up focusing more on the style than on the content of the message. Those not employing this style may misinterpret the rationale behind the emotion. Women, African Americans, Latino Americans, Asian Americans, Native Americans, those moderately educated, those from the southern and western regions of this country, and those not at the upper end of the socioeconomic scale are some of the cocultures that generally tend to use this style.

The *detached speaker style* is the fourth style. A speaker who uses this style will discuss all issues with calmness and objectivity and may be perceived by some as a speaker who can weigh all the factors impersonally. This style is not as compelling to listeners, but it also contains nothing to distract them from the process of listening. Those from the eastern and midwestern regions of this country, men, those who are highly educated, and those higher on the socioeconomic scale are some of the cocultures that generally use this style.

The fifth style is known as the *direct speaker style.* This style is highly reliant on the verbal coding system. A speaker who uses it conveys his or her message through explicit statements and places little reliance on contextual factors such as timing, situation, and nonverbal communication. The strength of the direct style is its clarity of communication, but this depends on using the same verbal coding system as the listeners. Some listeners, however, may perceive a double bind. A *double bind* is a situation where the words and nonwords don't exactly match, causing doubt about the speaker's honesty. Men, easterners, those who are highly educated, midwesterners, and those on the higher end of the socioeconomic scale are examples of cocultures that often use this style.

Our final style is the *indirect speaker style.* This style places heavy emphasis on nonverbal communication. Both words and nonwords are used to convey the message. Contextual cues such as suggestion and implication, along with nonverbal behavior, are important to this style. The weaknesses of this style are the possible misinterpretations of nonverbal cues and the need for high listener concentration. Though neither the verbal coding system nor the nonverbal coding system is identical for all users of the American English language, the verbal coding system has a more common framework than the nonverbal coding system. The strength of the indirect speaker style is that it may often provide greater motivation to listen to the message. Southerners, women, Native Americans, westerners, Asian Americans, those who are moderately educated, Latino Americans, those not at the higher end of the socioeconomic scale, and African Americans are some cocultures that often employ this style.

Which styles apply to you? Do you structure communication in a linear or circular fashion? Would your delivery style be characterized as passionate or calm? Does the format of your communicative messages rely more on the verbal coding system or the nonverbal coding system? Yes, you can use more than one of these styles. In fact, most people do. For example, I tend to be circular, attached, and indirect as a speaker/communicator, but I can shift to any style that I need, depending on the audience to whom I speak. This ability to shift styles takes time to develop and is easier for an experienced speaker than for a novice. Novice speakers can aid their causes by learning to compensate for some of the weaknesses and playing to the strengths of their natural styles.

Chapter 6: Communication Situations: The Speaker and Audience Deconstructed

With self-analysis completed, the speaker's next step must be to analyze the people to whom he or she will be speaking. An *audience analysis* involves gathering relevant demographic and attitudinal information about the audience and using that information to adapt the message in order to achieve the greatest impact. In public speaking, one size does not fit all. A competent public speaker will seek to adapt the message to the specific audience; this increases the chances for success. Let us examine the methods and factors surrounding an audience analysis.

There are four commonly used methods of gathering information about an audience. Not all of them are suited to all speakers and all situations. The first method is called *systematic observation,* and the information is gathered by simply eyeballing the audience. Very experienced speakers and speakers not using manuscripts may use this method. Since systematic observation is done just prior to addressing the audience, an experienced speaker would likely be better at dealing with the uncertainty involved in last-minute adaptation. A speaker who is speaking from a manuscript usually can make little last-minute adaptation; thus, this is not a good method of gathering audience information for speakers using that type of delivery. Though you may sometimes be forced to use this method, it does limit the types of information that can be provided. When we consider the factors involved in an audience analysis, see if you can figure out what types of information can be determined by systematic observation with relative certainty.

Conversation is the second method of gathering audience information. It is often used when the speaking situation is a part of a social situation such as a banquet, a dinner, or a cocktail party. Since the speech usually comes toward the end or in the middle of the social situation, the speaker can use the time before the speech to mingle with the audience and converse. Again, this method is better for those who have a good deal of experience at adapting their messages quickly and just prior to speaking. With enough time, the speaker can get a sense of some of the audience's attitudes in general and even about the speaker's topic in particular.

Like the previous two methods, the third method, a *show of hands*, will require quick adaptation, but this method becomes part of the presentation. Whenever the speaker gets to a point where he or she feels that specific information is needed to help determine how to proceed, the speaker asks a question and requests a verifiable response such as raising one's hand. Here the speaker uses the audience's responses to help figure out which approach is best. This method is definitely not for the inexperienced or for manuscript speakers.

The final method of directly gathering audience information is the *survey.* Although the survey would likely provide the most specific information, it is limited to situations where the audience was a known particular group of people. It is also limited to situations where there is plenty of time in advance to conduct the survey, gather and analyze the results, and plot adaptation strategies. If you are speaking to a particular organization, for example, a written survey could be distributed to the membership well in advance. Leaders within the organization could be used to help the speaker accomplish this. Though the survey can give the speaker excellent information (both demographic and attitudinal), it is rare that all the needed variables come together to allow a speaker to do this. Most of the time, the speaker has to rely on information provided by a contact person (usually the person who has invited the speaker to speak). Nevertheless, we will spend some time learning how to construct a competent survey. Even if it is a method the speaker will never use, the knowledge teaches the speaker what kinds of information are needed and what kinds of questions must be asked.

There are also two indirect methods of obtaining information that could be relevant to your audience. If you are addressing a specific group (like the members of a social, civic, or business club), there may already be *specific accumulated statistical data* available about them. Some organizations keep very thorough records on their membership; it never hurts to ask what is available. If no specific information is available and if there is no possibility of gathering relevant information, the speaker can turn to *general statistical data.* Using current opinion polls and the like won't give you the best information, but at least it provides a starting point.

From audience analysis types we move on to *audience analysis factors.* Ideally, the two major types of information that you hope to obtain from an audience analysis are *demographic information* and *attitudinal information.* Demographic factors can include such elements as the size of the audience, its gender composition, its racial composition, the audience's general educational level, and its general socioeconomic status. These demographic factors and the gross generalizations that go with them can help a speaker develop strategies applicable to the specific audience.

Knowing the *size* of the audience helps the speaker determine delivery strategies and decide on what types of audiovisual support to use. If, for example, the speaker has an intimate audience (defined as a situation where everyone in the audience can see the speaker and the speaker can see all the audience members), all forms of physical delivery become important and should be rehearsed. However, if the speaker has a huge audience and does not have the benefit of big screen projection, most physical forms of delivery become less important. The speaker's vocalics (use of pitch, rate, and volume) become crucial delivery elements. Since electronic vocal projection is likely a must in this situation, the speaker will have to learn how best to use whatever type of electronic vocal projection system has been made available. By the way, most speakers never face a huge audience. Most speeches in this country are presented in intimate audience situations.

The *sex* or gender breakdown of the audience is important to the speaker for several reasons. Here are some generalizations: A predominantly male audience is more impressed by, more captivated by, and more influence by a tightly structured, no-frills presentation. An audience with more females is more impressed by a presentation that provides both the facts and the human element involved in the topic. It is also important to note that if you are not of the same sex as most of the members of your audience, you will have to work harder to attain a good level of credibility. Perhaps you should review the speaker style information since much of it can be applied here and with the other audience analysis factors as well.

Like sex, the audience's *race*/racial makeup plays a role in credibility. Generally speaking, speakers of the same race as most of the audience will be given a higher level of credibility. However, there is an important exception to this rule. If the speaker's race is relevant to the topic, audiences of different races are apt to assign a higher level of credibility to the speaker despite racial differences between speaker and audience. For example, an African American speaker who is speaking about kwanza to a racially different audience would likely be assigned a higher level of credibility than a speaker of the same race as most of the audience.

The *age* of the audience can be a very pertinent factor for a speaker to know. Generally speaking, younger audiences are more malleable in the hands of a good rhetorician than older audiences. However, the Broom and Selznik study suggested that a speaker should also factor in the impact of the topic on the age group. When the topic can have potentially negative impacts on the age group in question, that group becomes very resistant to manipulative rhetoric. When the topic can have potentially negative impacts on another age group but not on the age group in question, the unaffected age group is fairly susceptible to manipulative rhetoric.

An audience's *educational level* gives the speaker strategic information. A more educated audience may be resistant to common rhetorical strategies, but they are most affected by the presentation of new information or by unique slants on existing information according to the Newcombe study.

The *socioeconomic status* of an audience invites two gross generalizations. The higher the socioeconomic level of the audience, the more resistant it will be to rhetorical advocacy for change. The lower the audience's socioeconomic level, the less resistant it will be to rhetorical advocacy for change.

Attitudinal factors involved in the process of audience analysis include the audience's political philosophy, the audience's religious philosophy, the attitude that the audience might have toward the speaker, and the attitude that the audience might have toward the speaker's topic.

Political philosophy is no longer an assessment of political party affiliation. Instead, the terms *liberal, conservative,* and *moderate* are the keys. Knowing how an audience might perceive itself, in terms of political philosophy, can give a speaker insight into how the audience might react to the speaker's style, various rhetorical strategies, and maybe even the speaker's topic.

The audience's *religious philosophy* is a matter of discerning affiliations. The knowledge of religious affiliation can be useful in helping the speaker to avoid rhetorical approaches that might run contrary to and offend certain religious affiliations. Though both political philosophy and religious philosophy are attitudinal factors, they can often be obtained by using a simple demographic audience analysis form.

The audience's *attitude toward the speaker* is the second most important piece of information that a speaker can possess. Unfortunately, this information is the most difficult to obtain. Unless the speaker is involved in an ongoing set of rhetorical encounters or is otherwise engaged with most of the members of the audience, there will probably be no cohesive or reliable reaction to the speaker by the audience beyond an initial knee-jerk response. However, some of the demographic data gathered may allow the speaker to make certain reasonable conjectures.

The audience's *attitude toward the topic* is the single most important piece of information that a speaker can possess. Most written surveys focus on this issue. Usually a series of emotionally charged topic statements and a Likert bipolar attitude scale are used in the survey to determine the audience's attitude toward the topic and the relative strength of that attitude.

Selznick, Philip. *The Commutarian Persuasion. 2002*

Broom, Leonard, Selznick, and Broom, Dorothy. *The Essential Sociology, 1984.*

Newcombe, N. and Arnkoff, D. B. *Ye Effects of Speech Style and Sex on Person Perception. Journal of Personality and Social Psychology, 1979. 37,.*

Communication Situations: Anxiety

First, we will explore the process of communication anxiety; then we will examine coping mechanisms that the less experienced public speaker can use to deal with communication anxiety.

Communication anxiety is simply a physical response to an anxiety-producing public performance situation. The process begins in the brain, which determines that there is a need for a special response to the approaching situation. A message from the brain is sent to the body urging the body to prepare for this situation. Unfortunately, the body has a universal response to all anxiety-producing situations. That response is known as the *fight-or-flight syndrome*. As far as the body is concerned, there is no difference between the anxiety experienced when facing off against a hungry, angry grizzly bear and when talking in front of a group of people. The fight-or-flight response is used for both. Of course, this response seems more applicable in the grizzly bear situation, where running or fighting makes sense; running away from or fighting with an audience does not. However, remember that the purpose of the fight-or-flight syndrome is simply to get the body ready to face whatever may occur.

The following major symptoms will give you an idea of how the process works. A message is received by the adrenal glands, two small glands located just above the kidneys; they respond by secreting large amounts of a very powerful hormone called *adrenaline*. The adrenaline in the bloodstream causes the heart to beat slightly faster. Though often imagined as being a major increase, the reality is that the heart will beat no faster than it will when running in place for one minute. As the body increases its functioning level, an unexpected oxygen debt is created. The panic response to this oxygen debt is one of the few noticeable (to an audience) symptoms of communication anxiety; most of the symptoms of communication anxiety are much more noticeable to the speaker than to the audience. Once the oxygen debt has set in, there will be a slight gasping of air (panic response) so that the breathing process can function properly. Since there is no physical exertion to cause the oxygen debt, speakers often exaggerate the symptom. It is not hyperventilation, and it is not asphyxiation. It is merely a temporary situation until the body adjusts to the need for greater oxygen intake.

Now another message is sent to the body that tells it to shut down all unnecessary functions. Any function that does not help the body get ready to face the anxiety-producing situation is temporarily halted. Chief among those suspended functions is digestion. Digesting food employs many resources; large quantities of blood are held in the abdominal walls to carry nutrients to other parts of the body. This is not particularly useful when getting ready to deal with anxiety. So, digestion is suspended, and whatever food is in the body remains in a nondigested state until communication anxiety passes. The blood resource will be redirected to other parts of the body where it can be better used. Ironically, it is the redirection of this blood that often causes a noted symptom of communication anxiety. This symptom is often called *butterflies*. Often a light and airy sensation, sometimes described as a "sinking" feeling, it is experienced in the stomach. Many interpret the symptom as nausea, but it is simply the rapid exit of blood from abdominal walls. That blood is being sent to the brain, the larger muscles of the arms, and the larger muscles of the legs.

The blood traveling to the brain may generate a flush along its journey. This usually occurs only in persons with fair skin and surface-oriented blood vessels. The blood traveling to the arms and legs, along with the adrenaline it contains, will lodge in the large muscles of the arms and legs. Those large muscles exist in antagonistic pairs. One set is used to contract, and one set is used to relax. The muscle used for contraction is equal in strength to the muscle used for relaxation. The adrenaline in the blood triggers both sets of muscles to react simultaneously. Since neither muscle can overpower the other, the speaker will experience a slight tremor in the hands and arms as well as a weak and wobbly feeling in the legs. This is not caused by cowardice; it is caused by two sets of muscles fighting each other. Despite whatever the speaker may perceive, these tremors are not visible to an audience. However, should the speaker add additional stress to the muscles in an effort to hide the tremors, they can become visible. In Chapter 8, you will learn how to make the tremors disappear completely.

The final major symptom of communication anxiety is an increase in body temperature. As the body increases its functioning level, it will naturally heat up. And, as we all know, when the body heats up, it will try to cool itself. Perspiration is a minor way that the body cools itself. The principal method of cooling is to directly expel heat into the air. The body will eliminate heat at three major sites—the top of the head, the soles of the feet, and the palms of the hands. Since hair, hats, shoes, and socks normally cut down on the amount of heat that can be eliminated from the top of the head and the soles of the feet, the main avenue of heat elimination is the palms of the hands. Heat emitted from the surface of the hands into a moisture-laden atmosphere will cause the moisture to condense on the surface of the hands. This can create a cold, clammy, sticky feeling on the palms.

The process described above deals only with the major symptoms of communication anxiety. These are symptoms that are usually common to most speakers. However, there are also many minor symptoms that, due to genetic differences among people, are less common. Some speakers may notice a flushing. This blush is caused by blood as it travels to the larger muscles of the arms, the legs and the brain. If you have fair skin and/or surface-oriented blood vessels, the blood's journey is visible. If you have a darker complexion and/or deep-oriented blood vessels, the blood's trip will not be visible. Some speakers experience a sense of impending urination, but find they do not really have to go. Muscle constriction in the bladder area produces that symptom. Some speakers experience waterfalls (too much saliva), and others experience too little saliva (dry mouth). Both symptoms are cause by muscle constrictions around the saliva glands. For waterfalls, the only thing to do is to keep swallowing the excess saliva. For dry mouth, speakers often have water at hand to keep the oral cavity moist. If you have other minor symptoms of communication anxiety, ask your instructor about them. Perhaps there is an explanation as to why the symptom occurs, and there may even be something you can do to alleviate the symptom.

Coping with communication anxiety requires an understanding of the process; it also requires a good mental attitude and practice. A good mental attitude means that the speaker focuses on the belief that he or she can succeed in the public speaking situation. It is a positive self-fulfilling prophecy. By contrast, a negative focus can lead to speaker failure in the same situation.

Practice has never made anyone perfect, but practicing can create a hedge against communication anxiety. The more a speaker practices, the more he or she builds confidence in facing the public speaking situation. The best form of practice for a public speaker is to practice in front of real people. By doing this, the speaker becomes accustomed to human variables. Getting accustomed to the reactions of people in your visual field while talking is important. Practicing alone in front of a mirror or in front of your pets does not help you to become accustomed to human variables. The little things that people do (mostly out of habit) while listening don't seem little when you are the one standing in front of them. The more you practice in front of people, the less likely you are to be greatly affected by them.

We have given the speaker, the first element of the public speaking situation, some consideration, and it is now time to turn our attention to the other major element in the public speaking situation—the audience. We will examine the audience as *listeners* and as *questioners*. Often, novice public speakers make the mistake of perceiving the audience as the enemy, but the competent public speaker will perceive it more realistically. The competent public speaker will perceive the audience as an obstacle. The audience isn't an intentional obstacle. In fact, audiences want the speaker to succeed; they would rather be part of a successful communicative situation than part of a failure. You'll learn more about this aspect of audience behavior in Chapter 8.

Unintentionally, however, the audience is an obstacle to a public speaker's success. The prime factor in considering the audience as an obstacle in a public speaking situation is *the audience's inability to listen well.* Americans are among the poorest listeners in the world, according to most listening studies. This is due primarily to the inability of Americans to remain focused on a single stimulus.

When it comes to the process of listening, Americans are better at some forms than others. Americans are good at most forms of social listening, but they are less successful at informational listening. Social listening forms (see Chapter 2) don't usually require a high level of concentration, and the listener is not expected to store the information for future use. Informational listening requires high, intense, and ongoing concentration levels, as well as information storage for future use. On average, the typical American has an informational listening capacity of 10 to 15 percent. This means that only 10 to 15 percent of most messages is processed to an acceptable level of understanding; the rest of most messages is lost. Unless the public speaker takes specific steps to raise this low listening level, most of his or her message will not reach the intended listener. We will discuss some of the strategies used to help increase low listening levels in Chapter 9.

In addition to being an unintentional obstacle to the public speaker as listeners, individuals in the audience *can sometimes be an intentional obstacle as questioners* in the question-and-answer period that often follows most public speaking situations. Even as individual questioners, the most dangerous obstacle they present to a speaker might be an unintentional one. Let's examine the five typical types of audience questioners.

First, there is the *hostile questioner*, who is mistakenly thought to be the most dangerous. The hostile questioner may be motivated by something the speaker said, by a dislike of the speaker, or just by having had a bad day. Regardless of the motive, the hostility is evident in both the wording and tone of the question. A competent public speaker knows that the worst thing to do is to respond with equal or greater hostility. If two people in a public speaking situation are behaving badly and one person is part of a group while the other is not, the group, in this case the audience, will tend to side with one of its own. However, if the speaker maintains a pleasant demeanor and greets the questioner's hostility with kindness in both wording and tone, the audience will likely align with the speaker.

Second is the *trapper questioner*, whose goal is to trap the speaker into agreeing with some idea that runs contrary to the ideas of the speech. Since the trapper questioner is trying to lure the speaker into a trap with a series of questions, the speaker must learn to look ahead to determine where this person is going. Perhaps the best tactic in dealing with this type of questioner is to learn not to answer in absolute terms; qualifying answers is a must.

Third, there is the *confusing questioner*. This person often just wants to participate in some way, so he or she will ask a question. The question, however, isn't well thought out. It will likely ramble, giving the person more time, and it won't make much sense. Here the best tactic is to, in effect, "make up your own question and answer it." The phrase "if you mean . . . then . . ." can aid you greatly, and this method will allow you to give additional information to the audience. The questioner is usually pleased that he or she was able to contribute, and the situation is ended.

The fourth type of questioner is the *final jeopardy questioner*. This person's motivation is to show the audience how brilliant and knowledgeable he or she is. The type of question that this audience member usually asks is one that could stump even the most seasoned expert and usually deals with unimportant, trivial elements of the topic. The best tactic is to simply admit that you do not know the answer. No reasonable audience will expect you to know everything, and not knowing will not harm your credibility with them. Offering to search for the answer and to let the questioner know once the answer is found is sufficient for most audiences. However, trying to fake an answer could get you into *ethos* trouble. Since this questioner will likely know the answer, faking an answer only gives him or her the opportunity to diminish you credibility.

The final and most deadly type of questioner is the *helpful questioner*. If you haven't properly conducted your research or if you haven't kept up with current information changes, this could be the death knell for your *ethos* with the audience. The helpful questioner doesn't mean to damage your credibility; like the confusing questioner, he or she just wants to participate by adding information to what has been said. Unfortunately, if the information that the helpful questioner adds conflicts with yours, you could be in trouble. The helpful questioner generally uses statements such as "I have been reading a book/article by the foremost expert(s), who say something very different." Then the questioner elaborates on the information. This situation is best avoided by being thorough and current in your research.

Now that you have some general information about the roles of the speaker and audience in a public speaking situation, we can consider other areas of knowledge that will be beneficial to a public speaker.

Communication Situations: Message Delivery

In an intimate audience setting, delivery is very important. Competent delivery skills can help overcome audience inattention and even some poor listening habits. Delivery is important to all speaker styles, but some speaker styles are more reliant on delivery concepts than others are. First, we will examine the four different forms of delivery. Then we will explore what constitutes effective speaker delivery.

Impromptu delivery is the first form of delivery. It involves speaking without prior preparation and without the benefit of any notes. Although experience and self-confidence make impromptu delivery less intimidating, this form can increase the symptoms of communication anxiety in the novice public speaker. Job interviews are really impromptu speaking situations.

The second delivery form, *memorized* delivery, is rare. Except in competitive speaking situations, it is generally not used. A memorized speech affords the speaker time to research the topic and to write and rewrite the speech until it is just as the speaker wants. Then the speaker need only commit the speech to memory.

Human memory is imperfect, and it can fail even the best speakers who possess the most common memory system, which is known as a *DMS* (dependent memory system). People with this type of memory system memorize in a word-for-word or line-for-line dependent fashion. Since in this system every word or phrase is a key for remembering the following word or phrase, the loss of one key word or phrase means that everything after it will be lost. Only extensive rehearsal over time can build a hedge against memory failure, but this is not foolproof. A very tiny percentage of speakers possess an *IMS* (independent memory system). For them, reciting from memory is almost like reading from a computer screen. Even if a word, phrase, or line is missing from the screen, the speaker can still determine what comes after it.

Manuscript delivery, the third type, is the most difficult form of delivery to execute competently. As with memorized delivery, the speaker has the opportunity to research the topic, write and rewrite the message, and rehearse the presentation. So, why is manuscript

Chapter 8: Communication Situations: Message Delivery

delivery so difficult to execute well? The principal obstacle is the audience. Adults do not like having someone read to them. In addition, mistakes made by a speaker reading from a manuscript are magnified greatly in the minds of an unforgiving audience. Really good manuscript speakers have exceptional delivery skills; unfortunately, very few exceptional manuscript speakers exist. Manuscript speaking has become very popular in the world of business and industry. Often these situations require manuscript speaking as a protection against litigation. Legal departments approve manuscripts, and if the agents of the business goes beyond the approved manuscript, they may be on their own. We will examine the special skills required of a manuscript speaker after discussing delivery skills in general.

The final form of delivery is *extemporaneous* delivery. This involves speaking from *brief* notes—only a word or phrase outline. The outline serves as a road map, placing the information in order. The speaker supplies the specific words as he or she would in an ordinary conversation. Extemporaneous delivery is the most adaptable form. Since the speaker is not tied to a specific set of words, he or she can adapt the message to the audience at hand. The speaker has the option of adding or subtracting examples and/or expanding or contracting whole segments of the presentation based on audience feedback. However, unlike impromptu delivery, extemporaneous delivery gives the speaker time to prepare. The speaker can research, but *the speaker does not write out a speech at any time with this form of delivery*. Instead, the speaker will organize his or her thoughts and figure out how the message should appear. Using this mental organizational process, the speaker constructs a word or phase outline as a reminder of the order of things in the presentation.

Now that we have an idea about the types of delivery available to speakers, let's explore effective delivery characteristics.

Enthusiasm can best be defined as the appearance of excitement regarding both the opportunity to address the audience and the speaker's specific topic. Enthusiasm is one of the mainstays of the attached delivery style, and it has the ability to compel audience attention to the point that most minor delivery errors go unnoticed by the audience. Enthusiasm may be a factor in the perception of *ethos* that the audience has about the speaker.

At this point, we should discuss a very important concept in the public speaking situation. The *reflective principle* indicates that audiences want speakers to succeed. Since audience members do not want to be part of a failed communicative event, they are willing to do their part to help the speaker succeed. To contribute to the success of the situation, an audience needs nonverbal direction from the speaker. Whatever nonverbal attitude the speaker conveys to the audience will be reflected back to the speaker. If the speaker gets excited about the topic, the audience can get swept up in the flood of excitement as well. Unfortunately, the reflective principle means that speaker's negative attitudes can be reflected back as well. If the speaker appears bored, the audience may also adopt that attitude. All the major nonverbally expressed emotions can be included here. If you have ever wondered how a group of people could be incited to riot by a speaker, you now have a clearer idea of how this could happen.

Sincerity is often difficult to define. The use of terms such as *honesty* and *trustworthiness* doesn't provide the full picture. Perhaps the best way to define sincerity is to say that it is the appearance that the speaker really wants to talk with the audience and treats the audience as an important part of the communicative situation. Sincerity is critical to the success of the detached speaker style. Sincerity may be a factor in the perception of *ethos* that the audience has about the speaker.

An erect *posture* can contribute to a positive perception of speaker credibility. In addition, standing straight, as opposed to adopting a more relaxed posture, aids in the breathing process. It can eliminate the speaker's need to gasp for air.

Stance, knowing how to place the feet, is important for two reasons. First, the speaker who stands with one foot slightly behind the other has balanced his or her body weight. This speaker will look comfortable and confident in the situation. By contrast, the speaker adopting an open or closed parallel placement of the feet will not have balanced body weight. This speaker is likely to engage in swaying motions or minor two-stepping to keep the body weight balanced. This movement without purpose makes the speaker seem uncomfortable and not very confident in the situation. Second, the speaker who places one foot slightly behind the other won't trip over his or her own feet when moving. Since communication anxiety sends a good deal of blood to the brain and since that blood is laden with adrenaline, nerve synapses may misfire, double fire, triple fire, and so on. This means that if the feet are parallel, both could simultaneously receive the command to move; both could try and execute that command at the same time. Unlike having one foot slightly behind the other, which would block simultaneous action, both feet are free to try to move at the same time in the parallel stance. The result would be a speaker falling over his or her own feet, which would not increase credibility.

In an intimate speaking situation, one of the most difficult delivery concepts for a novice public speaker to master is *movement,* which refers to using the feet and legs to go from one location to another. Effective speaker movement should have three characteristics. It should be purposeful, it should be to and from a central location, and it should be balanced. Movement involves the nonverbal concept of *proxemics,* which deals with how space and distance are used as communicative variables. Reducing the distance between speaker and audience increases audience attention, andmovement in general changes the visual picture for the audience. Changing the picture causes the audience to focus and refocus; thus, higher levels of audience attention are acquired by the speaker. Now let's examine the three characteristics of effective speaker movement.

First, effective speaker movement should have *purpose.* A speaker shouldn't move just for the sake of moving; there should be a reason for it. Speakers should watch their audience carefully; as audience attention wanes, the speaker should move to help regain that attention. Additionally, some movement is needed to help ease the tension in the larger muscles of the legs, and the tremors and weakness associated with communication anxiety should dissipate as a result of this movement.

Second, effective speaker movement should be *to and from a central location.* In an intimate audience situation, a speaker should find the approximate center in front of the audience. All movement (both vertical and horizontal) should be away from and back to that center point. When a speaker moves from the center point, he or she should not immediately return to the center. Instead, the speaker should linger for a period of time in the new location. However, the speaker should not get stranded at any point away from that center spot.

Finally, effective speaker movement should be *balanced.* People are creatures of habit; they have a tendency to fall into patterns. One such pattern can involve movement. Some speakers may only move to their right and back, and some may only move to their left and back. However, the speaker executing balance in movement will make a conscious effort to compensate for movement in one direction by eventually, but not immediately, moving in the opposing direction. A movement to the far right eventually calls for a movement to the far left. This way the speaker doesn't seem to nonverbally favor one segment of the audience over any other.

The most common movement errors include no movement (which can lose audience attention), too much movement (which can also lose audience attention), and swaying (which is not an effective compromise and reduces credibility).

Gesticulation, the movement of hands and arms, is another tool a speaker can use to get, hold, and/or regain audience attention. Gesturing also reduces the stress in the larger muscles of the arms and decreases the tremors associated with communication anxiety. Gesticulation belongs in the nonverbal category known as *kinesics,* which deals with movement as a communicative form . There are three types of gesticulations. *Emblems* are gestures that generally communicate without the use of words. Waving goodbye to someone is an example of an emblem, as is holding up four fingers to represent the number 4. *Illustrators* are gestures that accompany words to enhance the process of communication. For example, a speaker talking about a fish that was caught might use his or her hands to specify the size of the fish. *Adaptors* are habitual gesticulative forms. Though adaptors don't intentionally communicate, these habits (like scratching the nose, tugging the ear, clicking the nails, playing with change in pockets, shuffling/twisting notes, etc.) multiply with the addition of stress. Sometimes a speaker's adaptive behavior, due to the effects of communication anxiety, may be costly to his or her *ethos.*

Executing effective gesticulation is easy. A speaker should gesture in a way that comes naturally. However, two modifications need to be made. First, gesticulation needs to be moved outward from the trunk of the body. Gesturing close to the trunk of the body is fine for conversation, but it does not have the visibility or impact needed when communicating with a group of people. Second, normal gestures have to be exaggerated slightly. Again, the purpose is to increase both visibility and impact on the communication recipients.

Eye contact is vital to a public speaker. It allows the speaker to perceive audience feedback, which is essential to adapting to the audience. Eye contact in our culture is associated with honesty. Lack of effective eye contact will likely have a negative impact on the audience's perception of the speaker's credibility. Effective eye contact means that the speaker makes every effort to distribute eye contact equally across the audience. It also means that the speaker tries to make everyone in the audience feel that at some point the speaker is talking to him or her. Speakers should not focus on one person or one segment of the audience. Nor should they fake eye contact or stare at the floor or ceiling. Finally, looking mostly at his or her notes or at audiovisual aids does not endear the speaker to the audience.

Facial expressions are more important to the indirect speaker style than to the direct speaker style. However, they have a degree of importance for all speakers. No one facial expression is always appropriate; speakers have to be careful to match. the facial expressions and the words. Inappropriate facial expressions (those that don't match the words), no facial expressions, and a lack of variety in facial expressions can all generate double binds.

The nonverbal area of *paralanguage* provides our last delivery characteristics. Paralanguage deal with how we make words sound (*vocal characteristics*) and the nonword sounds (*vocal differentiators*) that humans make. Vocal characteristics, or vocalics, include pitch, rate, and volume. *Pitch* deals with the highness or lowness given to the vocal tone of words. For example, we can express surprise or shock by responding in a higher pitch than normal, or we can express seriousness by responding in a lower pitch than normal. Thus, we can affect the perceived meaning of words by altering the pitch at which they are delivered. In addition, making conscious changes in the pitch at which we speak can help get, keep, and/or regain audience attention. *Rate* refers to the speed at which we delivery words. The dialectical region in which we live normally determines the normal rate at which we speak. The average rate of speech in the area in which we reside is around 165 to 175 words per minute. Varying that rate can affect the perception of the words used. A rapid rate, for example, could be perceived as a lack of desire to continue the process of communication; a very slow, deliberate rate could be perceived as a comment on the intelligence of the listener. Making intentional rate changes while delivering a speech can help keep, hold, and/or regain audience attention. *Volume* is the loudness or softness of tone used to deliver words. Both loud and soft volumes can be used to emphasize what the speaker is saying. How loudly or softly a word or phrase is delivered to an audience may affect how it is perceived. Deliberate changes in speaking volume can help get, hold, and/or regain audience attention.

When it comes to vocalics, the worst problem isn't a monotone (no changes at all) because monotones are very difficult to achieve either intentionally or unintentionally. The biggest problem that speakers have with vocal characteristics is the problem of *patterned speech*. Instead of making deliberate changes in pitch, rate, and volume, the speaker falls into a habitual pattern of making the same changes over and over again without any conscious input to the process. Patterned speech is difficult to listen to consistently. The heavy rhythm of the pattern lulls the audience into an inattentive state.

Vocal differentiators include special vocalizations and breakers. *Special vocalizations* include all the sounds that humans use to communicate various things. Examples include moans, groans, sighs, crying, and laughing. A person under stress may unconsciously produce these sounds. Communication anxiety carries with it enough stress to precipitate the "nervous giggle." If produced at an inappropriate time, this giggle can have a very negative effect on a speaker's *ethos*. *Breakers* are verbal disfluencies—sounds that simply disrupt the normal flow of speech. *Breakers are a normal part of human communication*; eliminating them completely from human speech is virtually impossible. Examples of these sounds include *um, ah, er,* and *uh*. Normally, these habitual sounds don't cause major problems. However, breakers are extremely sensitive to stress. This means that communication anxiety can cause the number of breakers to double, triple, or quadruple. At very high levels, breakers may be perceived as a sign that the speaker is being dishonest or is not knowledgeable. As communication anxiety ebbs, breakers will drop back to their normal level.

Now that we have explored the basic delivery concepts, let's examine the special adaptations a speaker will have to make with these concepts to competently execute manuscript delivery.

Speakers, regardless of their style, will need higher levels of *enthusiasm* and *sincerity*. Increased intensity here will help to compensate for an adult audience's dislike of having a speaker read to them.

Posture and *stance* increase in importance with manuscript delivery. It is essential that the speaker look both comfortable and confident. An erect posture here means being parallel with the speaker's lectern or podium; there should be little or no contact. Do not use the lectern to support yourself; it is there only to support the manuscript. Balanced body weight will keep you looking competent, and it will prevent you from inadvertently kicking the podium and creating a listening distraction.

Movement is virtually precluded because of the reliance upon the text. The most movement a speaker can reasonably execute is movement slightly to each side while, of course, maintaining his or her place in the manuscript with one hand.

Gesticulation is restricted to one hand and arm. At all times, a speaker should use one hand to follow the text to make sure that he or she doesn't lose the place in the manuscript. Getting lost in your own text diminishes your credibility. Gesturing only with one hand requires gesticulation to be well thought out and very deliberate.

Since maintaining *eye contact* with the audience is very important, a manuscript speaker has to work very hard to maintain adequate contact. Even more important, a manuscript speaker should look as if he or she really isn't reading the manuscript. Bobbing up and down between audience and text does not give the speaker the air of credibility that is needed. A speaker must become so familiar with the text that he or she can maintain substantial eye contact with the audience. More rehearsal time is needed for manuscript delivery than for any other delivery form.

Facial expressions play an even more important role in manuscript delivery than in other forms of delivery. When a speaker is reading to them, audiences are much keener on making sure that the words and nonwords match. Audience studies tell us that facial expressions are central to this determination of believability.

With movement and gesticulation diminished in ability, *pitch, rate,* and *volume* become the best tools that the speaker has to help get, keep, and/or regain audience attention. Intentional and carefully thought out vocalic changes are essential to help the speaker avoid the plague of audience inattention.

Communication Situations: Message Structure

For years, communication professors only taught a linear organizational structure. However, cultural awareness mandates that we include instruction on circular formats as well. With linear and circular styles both in mind, let's explore the four steps needed to put together a competent public speech. And remember, once you learn the process, it can and should be used with any type of speech you are constructing and with all delivery styles that you might use.

The first step in the process of structuring a speech is the construction of the *opening* or *introduction.* In oral communication, an introduction performs two critical functions; it attracts the audience and focuses its attention. Even though a speaker may stand and begin speaking, audience members are not necessarily listening. Listening studies tell us that it may take anywhere from thirty seconds to two minutes before a majority of audience members actually listen to the speaker. The audience may hear the speaker, but they aren't necessarily listening (processing information to a level of understanding). An effective oral introduction must either reduce the time before effective listening begins or fill that time with relevant but not critical information. It is not enough to simply attract attention; a good introduction/ opening must focus the audience's attention on the specific subject matter of the speech.

There are several ways that a speaker can open the presentation; we will focus on four of the most effective methods. The first two methods are the only ones that reduce the time before effective listening begins; the last two methods fill the time before effective listening begins with relevant but not critical information. *Reference to the audience* is considered the most effective method of gaining audience attention. This method gets the audience to listen faster than any other introductory form. To use it, a speaker begins by paying the audience a compliment. Since people like hearing nice things about themselves, listening levels rise in anticipation that more nice things will be said. However, it is not enough to pay the audience a compliment; the speaker must relate that compliment to his or her topic. The process of establishing a relationship between the compliment and the topic can be called *dropping an ego bomb.* In other words, the ego receives validation of some kind by continuing the listening process. For example, if a speaker tells an audience that they are an intelligent-looking group of people, he or she has used the compliment portion of this introductory form. Now the speaker must establish a relationship between the compliment and the topic for the ego bomb. The speaker can do this by telling the audience that intelligent people are interested in or concerned about the topic. Since the egocentric audience will want to believe they are intelligent and since, as they were told, intelligent people are concerned about/interested in the subject of the speech, they listen better in order to validate their self-image as intelligent people. Speakers must be careful to use this introductory form with great sincerity. If audiences perceive a lack of sincerity on the speaker's part, they may not listen well.

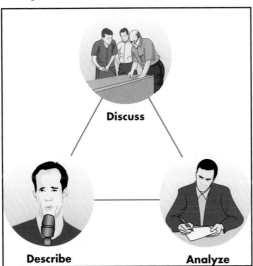

Another way of getting an audience's attention faster and reducing the time before effective listening begins is to use a *startling statement*. The startling statement uses shock value to capture the audience's attention. Of course, it must be related to the speaker's topic. For example, if a speaker told an audience that there was a good chance that four of them would not be alive tomorrow, members of that audience would likely have a high level of interest. If the speaker continued by telling the audience that this statement could be true because one out of every four persons dies in a traffic accident nearly every day on the highways of the United States, and if the speaker indicated that he or she wants to discuss traffic safety, then the speaker has fulfilled his or her obligation with regard to using the startling statement.

Of the forms a speaker can use to fill time before most audience members actually listen, two of the best are narrative forms and story forms. The purpose of filling the time with something of relevant interest is to help hold the attention of audience members who are listening. However, the most crucial information is delayed until the majority of audience members are paying attention.

Story and narrative forms are naturally seductive to listeners. When people hear the beginning of a story, they anticipate its middle. When people hear the middle of a story, they anticipate its end. Thus, narrative forms pull people into the listening process. The *literary reference* allows the speaker to retell a story (abbreviating and paraphrasing as necessary) from any form of literature (a short story, novel, movie, song/poem, etc.). For example, a speaker doing a presentation on individual retirement accounts might begin by retelling Aesop's fable of the grasshopper and the ant.

The *personal reference* is not a fictional story; it is something real that the speaker has experienced. The speaker tells a related personal story as a means of pulling the audience into the presentation.

Two other ways of filling the thirty-second to two-minute gaps between hearing and actual listening include reference to the subject and reference to the occasion.

Reference to the subject is the most commonly used introductory form. It allows the speaker to begin with information that is related to the main topic indirectly or subtly rather than directly or overtly. For example, a speaker giving an informative speech on the idea of a hydrogen-powered car could begin by discussing the high cost of fossil fuels (indirectly related) or changes in automobile designs over the years (indirectly related). Thus, the audience would hear related information for up to two minutes. Those who were listening from the beginning would have good additional information, and those who were not would not have missed the critical material that the speaker wanted them to have.

Reference to the occasion is the most specialized introductory form that we will consider. Its use is limited to speaking situations that grow out of an occasion. Examples include graduations, retirements, anniversaries, specific celebrations, and specific holidays. With this type of introduction, the speaker begins by talking about the occasion. Since people have gathered for the occasion, they will naturally have some interest in hearing about it. The speaker cannot and/or should not devote the entire speech to the occasion. However, before going on to the main purpose of the speech, the speaker should make sure to link the occasion to his or her major purpose. This form of introduction would work in a speech of introduction on the occasion of a graduation. Here is an example: "Graduates, parents, family members, faculty members, and administrators, I would like to thank you all for allowing me to share in this very special day. Each of you graduates has worked hard over the years to be here. Now, your parents, your siblings, your spouses, your friends, and the rest of your family have gathered to celebrate this special day with you. Today, you will take a major step toward your future. This step not only affects your future; it also affects America's future. If America is to remain the greatest nation in the world, it will be up to people like the graduates we see today to take on the political and economic challenges that face it." It should be evident to a listener that the speaker will be talking about either economic challenges facing the country or political challenges or both. Yet, remember that the speaker had to get the audience's attention by talking about the day and then lead the audience to the speech's focus by linking the celebration to the topic.

Before leaving this first step in the process of structuring a presentation, let us explore three forms of introduction that are used in oral communication out of a lack of knowledge: humor, a quotation, or a rhetorical question. Their use should be very limited or eliminated altogether.

An experienced public speaker knows that *humor* is the riskiest way to begin a speech. It is true that laughter exists in all cultures, but what stimulates that laughter varies widely from culture to culture, from coculture to coculture, and from person to person. This means that what you find funny may not amuse your audience. If the joke fails, listening may be extremely negatively affected. If an audience doesn't listen, the speaker cannot achieve his or her goal. You have often watched television and movie speakers search for that great joke. Keep in mind that these are fictional situations.

Failed humorous attempts in other parts of the speech are easier to recover from than those in the introduction. In the introduction, humor is a risk that you may not wish to take. Humor is a fine rhetorical tool for those who can make it work for them. Speakers with a great sense of comic timing and delivery or speakers with a great team of professional speech writers have a much easier time using humor than does the average speaker.

In written communication, a *quotation* or a *rhetorical question* is an acceptable way of beginning. In oral communication, it is not. Unless one is clairvoyant, the chances of choosing the right quotations with the right compelling quality are small. In oral communication, quotations best serve as supportive material. A rhetorical question, whose purpose is to get the audience to think but not to answer, can actually distract the audience from the process of listening. While the audience ponders the answer to question, the speaker continues; listening is not well served.

The second step in constructing a presentation is the *oral preview.* The oral preview is not exactly like a thesis statement used by a writer. In fact, it differs from the written thesis statement in three significant ways. First, there is a difference in *purpose.* Both indicate the subject matter, but an oral preview also tells the audience how to listen. By using *listening cue* words, the speaker is able to tell the subconscious mind, which is in charge of data storage, what kind of listening is required. *Social listening cue* words (e.g., *talk, tell, share, view*) tell the subconscious mind that information storage is not required, but *informational listening cue* words (e.g., *discuss, describe, explore, inform, explain, identify, analyze*) indicate that information storage is needed. A competent oral preview will employ either a social listening cue or an informational listening cue to indicate subtly to the listener's subconscious mind which type of listening is required. Generally speaking, personal narrative speeches, after-dinner speeches, and speeches of introduction use social listening cues. Informational speeches, persuasive speeches, and argumentative speeches use informational listening cues. An informational listening cue can be used in virtually any speaking situation, but social listening cues are limited to situations where information storage is not critical for speaker success.

The second difference between an oral preview and a written thesis statement is *placement.* Writers are encouraged to explore stylistic and structural alternatives. Some writers make the thesis the first sentence, some place it at the end, and some insert it somewhere in the middle. However, a competent speaker does not have reasonable structural alternatives. It would be illogical to place the oral preview, which tells the audience how to listen and what to listen to, before the introduction because that would involve telling them how to listen and what to listen to before gaining their attention. It also would not make sense to place the oral preview within or at the end of the speech. Why tell the audience what to listen to and how to listen after you have already delivered the information? Thus, the most logical place for an oral preview is immediately after the introduction and before the body of the speech.

The final difference between a written thesis and an oral preview is the *complexity* of the sentence structure. A written thesis statement can use a very complex sentence structure. A reader who doesn't fully understand it can read it as many times as are necessary to gain understanding. However, listeners do not have the opportunity to hear an oral preview over and over again until it is understood. Thus, an oral preview should have a very simple structure. The best oral previews are usually simple declarative sentences (e.g., "Let's examine the advantages of learning a foreign language" [information listening cue] or "I am going to tell you about my experiences as a small-business owner" [social listening cue]).

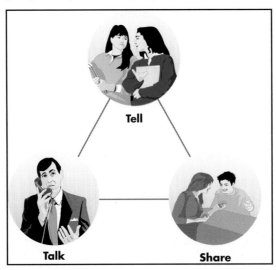

Tell

Talk   **Share**

Developing the *body of the speech* is the third step in the process of putting together a presentation. It is essential that the body be the third step. Many speakers would like to stand, say what they have to say, and sit, but that approach would work only if there were an audience filled with trained listeners. In every other situation, the introduction and preview must precede the body of the speech. Even when they arrive at this stage, speakers cannot just say whatever they want the audience to know. Since getting the audience to both understand and remember the message is normally crucial to the process, speakers have to know how to structure information to increase the chances for comprehension and retention. Thus, we must examine relevant information from the realm of *information theory*, which deals with the efficiency of passing information from person to person. We shall focus on one particular information theory, called the *big block information theory*, which will allow us to deal with both the *linear* and *circular* speaker styles. Remember that the linear speaker style moves directly from point to point within the framework of an explicitly stated idea. The circular style works within a framework of an idea that is implied or more subtly indicated. This style may employ narratives or stories that don't necessarily seem directly linked but do lead to a specific point.

The big block information theory states that listeners will likely remember more if information is presented in larger related chucks than if it is presented as individual units. Rather than presenting one fact after another in isolation, the speaker bundles related units of information together using a unifying framework; this makes it easier for listeners to both understand and remember the information. The rules associated with the big block information theory include limiting the number of blocks of information to seven and making each block of information independent of the other blocks.

Organizational patterns like *the chronological pattern, the cause-effect pattern, the problem-solution pattern, the topical pattern,* and the *spatial pattern* are the frameworks used by the big block information theory to bundle together information units.

Both linear style speakers and circular style speakers can employ the frameworks and the big block information theory, but each will use the tools differently. The *chronological pattern* organizes information in a time-related or sequential pattern. Thus, each block of information is a time unit or sequence step. A linear style speaker would likely organize the major point around a single sequence of occurrences, but a circular style speaker might juggle several different chronological narratives on the way to making a point.

The *spatial pattern*, sometimes called the *geographical pattern*, organizes information based on space relationships. Here, each block of information is determined by a physical relationship to a specific space. A circular style speaker would use several narratives that deal with geographical relationships; a linear style speaker would develop his or her point by dividing that point into related spatial blocks of information.

The *topical pattern* allows a speaker to take a very large subject and subdivide it into smaller areas. It also allows the speaker to choose from among the subdivisions according to the time available. Thus, each block of information is a subunit of a larger topic with which the speaker had to deal. A linear style speaker would use clearly delineated subtopics, but a circular style speaker would create stories around the subtopics.

To properly use the *cause-effect pattern*, the speaker should use only two blocks of information. One block should deal only with causes and the other block only with effects. A circular style speaker would likely have a series of narratives about causes followed by a series of narratives about effects leading to a point. The linear style speaker would deal with the causes of one situation before dealing with the effects of that situation.

Chapter 9: Communication Situations: Message Structure

Like the cause-effect pattern, the *problem-solution pattern* is often misused by comingling the two blocks of information. Speakers should work to keep the blocks of information independent of one another. The problem-solution pattern should have one block that deals only with the problem and one block that deals only with a single solution or multiple solutions. The linear style speaker would likely deal with one problem and with one or more solutions that mitigated or solved that problem. A circular style speaker would likely have narratives dealing with related problems and would move to possible ways of dealing with them.

One tool that speakers using both styles should employ to aid the listener is called *signposting*. This tool helps listeners to understand better and retain more information. Signposting uses the alphanumeric system to form a road map for listeners. Each signpost has a *preview* and a set of *flags*. The signpost preview can be the speech's preview, or it can be an independent preview placed inside the body of the speech. What the preview does is to tell the listener the number of information blocks that should be understood and retained. First, let's look at an example of a signpost preview that is also the speech's preview. If a speaker was giving a speech on poverty using a topical organizational pattern, the preview for the entire speech could be as follows: "Today, I would like to examine three aspects of poverty." The speech's preview tells the listener that there are three critical blocks of information that the listener should work to understand and remember. An example of an independent preview within the body of the speech might be found in a speech using the problem-solution pattern. After finishing the discussion of the problem, the speaker could preview multiple solutions as follows: "Now that we have explored the problem, I would like to explain two possible solutions." Again, the use of the preview (an independent preview this time) tells the audience that there are two important blocks of information to be understood and remembered.

The purpose of the flags is to announce the arrival of information that the speaker deems important for listener understanding and retention. Although the preview always employs a specific number, the flags can use numerals (1, 2, 3, etc.), letters of the alphabet (A, B, C, etc.), or numerical word equivalents (*first, second, third*, etc.). This process can help the audience better understand and remember only if the speaker uses the flags consistently. In other words, the speaker cannot start with one flag format and switch to another format in midstream (1, 2, C or A, B, 3 or first, second, C). Speakers also should not start the flagging process and then drop it. The word *next* is not a flag.

Admittedly, signposting is more natural for a linear style speaker than for a circular style speaker. However, signposting does not diminish the circular style's integrity, but it does help map the speaker's strategy for the linear listener.

Before leaving the body of the speech, we need to address the issue of oral style. Although a speaker should always think about these ideas, oral style is especially important in developing manuscript speeches. All too often, beginning speechwriters construct compositions instead of speeches. Compositions are meant to be read; speeches are meant to be heard. People do not generally write the way they speak. Written and oral communication differ greatly. It is often helpful for novice manuscript speakers to first dictate the manuscript speech into a tape recorder rather than writing it. This method will bring them closer to the way they talk rather than the way they write.

Let's examine eight significant differences between oral and written style. First, oral style uses *short, simple words*. Trying to impress a listener with your vocabulary won't win you points. Remember that the listeners have to understand the message using listening skills that are often poor. If the listeners do not comprehend the message, the speaker has simply wasted everyone's time. Since a speaker usually has no way of knowing what the listeners' vocabulary levels are, it is best to keep the vocabulary relatively simple to enhance understanding. Second, to stay within the bounds of oral style, a speaker should employ *short, simple sentences*. Again, the reasoning centers on understanding. The listener cannot head for a dictionary when words are not understood; also, unlike the reader, the listener cannot go back and reread long, complex sentences. Keeping sentences short and using simple sentence structures will help keep the listener a viable part of the communication process.

Third, *short, simple paragraphs* are part of oral style. The idea is still to keep information structured so that a listener can comprehend it. Word economy is important in oral communication. A speaker shouldn't use five hundred words when fifty words will get the message across. Fourth, an oral communicator should make *greater use of personal pronouns. I, you, me, us,* and *them* are commonly heard in conversations. Personal pronouns both specify and add a personal touch to communication. Unlike speakers, writers must often write not knowing who will read their work.

Fifth, a speaker should make *greater use of contractions.* Although contractions are not generally encouraged in formal written communication, there is no reason why speakers cannot employ them. Contractions are part of the standard vocabulary of most speakers; thus, using them helps to make a speech seem more like human conversation than written communication. Sixth, an oral communicator can make *greater use of appropriate slang expressions.* Although formal written communication avoids slang, oral communication encourages the use of any tools that clarify the message. However, oral communication also recognizes the limitations of slang in communicating. In oral communication, slang is defined as a group vocabulary difference. Differing age groups, occupational groups, racial groups, regional groups, and so on all have their own slang expressions. Using the slang of a group to communicate with that group may enhance the communication process. Using slang that does not fit the group may generate a communication breakdown.

Seventh, in oral communication a speaker must use *internal summaries.* Since we know that the average listener's ability to concentrate is very poor, internal summaries are useful to keep the listener both involved with the message and able to comprehend it. Finally, a writer writes for a general audience but a speaker targets a specific audience. An effective speaker makes a *direct adaptation to the audience.* Both while speaking and while constructing a speech, a speaker should have the audience uppermost in mind. Figuring out how something can best be communicated to a specific group of people is critical to the oral communicative process. In oral communication, the belief that "one size fit all" is simply false.

The fourth and final step in the process of putting together a speech is writing the *conclusion or ending.* A conclusion serves two vital purposes. It *brings a sense of completeness* to the speech, and it *leaves a favorable impression of the speaker* in the minds of the audience. Although each of the introductory forms can be refitted and used as a conclusion (with the exceptions of the quotation and perhaps humor), let's examine four effective ways of ending a speech.

First, we have the most common form of conclusion: the *summary.* Unfortunately, too many speakers confuse summarization with repetition. A true speech summary employs the process of restatement and uses no repetition. In restatement, the speaker analyzes his or her message to determine the most critical ideas—the ones the speaker most wants the audience to remember. The speaker finds a unique and brief way to encapsulate these ideas in a few memorable sentences.

Second, a speaker can end the speech by using a *challenge* or an *appeal.* When the speaker knows that the audience is comprised of egocentric and ego-secure people, the challenge can be used without hesitation. To end with a challenge, the speaker adopts a rhetorically superior posture to the audience and dares them to do something or achieve something. Unlike the challenge, the appeal requires an audience that tends to be humanitarian and empathetic. To close with an appeal, a speaker rhetorically assumes an inferior posture to the audience and pleads with them to respond in a particular way.

Third, the use of a *moral* or *lesson* is an effective way to close a speech. A speaker wrapping up his or her message by using the moral/lesson form will focus on the question "What can be learned from all of this?" This form of conclusion brings to light or reinforces some moral standard for the audience, or it teaches or reinforces some important life lesson.

The fourth and final form of conclusion is the *catch phrase*, which here would be comparable to a slogan. The idea is that the speaker finds a way to convert the essence of his or her message into a single sentence that is both compelling and memorable to the listener. Although a speaker can use or borrow from what already exists, an audience would likely be more impressed with a phrase that is new and unique.

These four steps are the same steps (in the same order) that a speaker should use in putting together a speech. Regardless of the type of speech, these steps will help to structure it successfully and create a climate where audience comprehension and retention can occur.

Communication Situations: Message Credibility

Speakers need *ethos* or credibility to help them get their message accepted by the audience. Various types of credibility are available to speakers. Let's review them before we move on to other aspects of credibility.

First, there is *antecedent ethos* or credibility developed prior to the actual communication. It can come from an established reputation (e.g., the well-known consumer advocate Ralph Nader) and is called *reputational antecedent ethos*. Antecedent *ethos* can also come from the situation {*situational antecedent ethos*}. Talking to a previously unknown doctor in his or her office would be an example.

Due to the reputation or situation, the receiver would automatically grant a level of credibility to the speaker. Antecedent *ethos* can be either positive or negative.

Second, there is *present ethos,* which is credibility based on the actual communication (what is said as well as how it is said). In essence, a speaker who develops present *ethos* does so by borrowing credibility from supportive materials used. Since many speakers (like students in a classroom) have credibility that is perceived as only equal to or less than that of most of their listeners, they must borrow credibility from other sources that have more credibility with the listeners, Though an audience might not believe information if you presented it as your own original thought, they might believe it if it came from a source (an interview with a recognized expert or a respected journal, Internet source, newspaper or news magazine) they believed in and/or respected.

The benefit of using supportive material can best be explained by understanding the *halo effect.* Though the speaker may borrow credibility only to make one or two issues more believable to the audience, the end result is that the speaker's overall credibility is enhanced; this is the halo effect. However, sources with credibility problems can produce a negative halo effect for speakers who use them. (Just think, some of you may have been citing sources in written communication for years, believing that the only reason to do so was to meet the requirements of the assignment. In reality, this process, wherever used, is designed to increase credibility.)

This borrowed credibility can come from two types of sources. One of them is a primary source—direct contact (an interview) with a recognized expert. With a primary source of information, the *grapevine effect* (the unintentional distortion of information as it passes from one individual's perception to another's) would have only a minor impact. This impact is minor because the information goes only from the expert to you, creating a very short chain of unintentional distortion.

By contrast, secondary sources, which are nondirect contact and nonperson sources (professional journals, Internet sites, news magazines, newspapers, videotapes, audiotapes, etc.), are highly affected by the grapevine effect. The process of editing, which adds the perceptions of others, makes secondary sources highly subject to the grapevine effect. However, the average audience member is probably not aware of this unintentional distortion. He or she would likely believe that an article printed in a newspaper, for example, was exactly what the reporter had originally written.

We can further differentiate supportive material by examining its three major categories—factual data, opinion data, and statistical data.

Initially, we should consider *factual data*. We should start by recognizing that the *standard definition* of a fact and the *operational definition* of a fact are different. For a speaker, a fact is not something he or she knows to be true or can prove beyond almost all doubt to listeners (the standard definition). For a speaker, a fact is that which a majority of the listeners will accept as true without major controversy (the operational definition or working definition, which is the one we really use in day-to-day life). A fact, in communication, is most often established through common knowledge. Thus, when a speaker is dealing in the realm of common knowledge, he or she does not need to borrow credibility to be perceived as believable. However, when working outside the realm of common knowledge, a speaker is best served by borrowing credibility from sources that the audience would likely find more credible than the speaker.

Opinion data is just someone's opinion; it is not fact and is not statistically based. Not all opinions have the same degree of credibility, and not all opinions have credibility that can be borrowed.

For example, *lay opinion*, the average person's opinion, is the weakest form of opinion data. A speaker should not attempt to borrow credibility from this source since it has no more credibility than the speaker has. Unlike lay opinion, *expert opinion* is a good source of credibility. Audiences, generally speaking, feel that someone who is trained and/or experienced in an area has knowledge beyond that of the ordinary person. Though it does not seem as logical as the idea behind expert opinion, *public opinion*, the collected opinion of the masses, tends to be a very powerful source of credibility. Because most audiences do not like to feel out of step with everyone else, they find public opinion quite compelling.

Finally, there is *statistical data*. As a speaker, you should be aware of the fact that audiences are generally intimidated by numbers, but as a listener, you should always remember that statistics are only numerical generalizations. Since most listeners do not fully understand statistical manipulation, they tend to see the numbers as being beyond dispute. Thus, speakers can often greatly enhance their credibility by borrowing from statistical sources.

Having dealt with the forms and sources of support, our next step is to discuss how to employ supportive material in oral communication. It is important to keep in mind that using supportive material in oral communication is different from using it in written communication. In an oral communication situation, there are five things to remember about using supportive material.

First, determine if or where proof is needed to build credibility. For example, the speaker who is outside the realm of common knowledge needs to borrow credibility from sources of information that have *ethos* with the audience, which will then accept the sources and believe the point being made by the speaker.

Second, cite the sources of the borrowed information. Since credibility comes from the source of the information and not from the information itself, the speaker must name the source to acquire its credibility.

Third, the qualifications of primary or human sources of information must be provided by the speaker. Not every expert is a household name; a speaker will need to provide the specific qualifications (not just titles) of the human sources he or she uses. This qualification process must give the listener justification for believing the source, the information, and the speaker.

Fourth, the speaker should state when the information became available. Since humans do not talk like the bibliographies and footnotes in written communication, time is handled in a more conversational way. For example, it would be acceptable to refer to "an issue of last week's *Journal Star*" as opposed to citing the specific date, volume, issue, and page.

Fifth and finally, a speaker must integrate the supportive material into the natural flow of communication. By using conversational transitions, a speaker can make the use of supportive material sound conversational and not segmented, as it is in written communication.

Since we now know that not all supportive material will help build speaker credibility, our last focus will be on making the best choices regarding where to borrow and not to borrow credibility. For this, we need to understand the *tests of logical adequacy*. In evaluating supportive material, these tests can be used by any speaker to make wise choices. Not every source will do; a competent speaker must examine how his or her audience might react to the source being considered. In addition, the tests of logical adequacy can be used by listeners to evaluate what they hear and to avoid being easily deceived. Let's examine these tests.

First, there is the *test of reliability*. This test is used to make sure that the sources used do not have a reputation for error. The reliability an audience will grant any source depends on the source and the audience. However, a speaker can make educated guesses based on audience credibility studies. Here is a rank ordering (from highest believability to lowest) of general source categories and examples:

1. Professional journals (e.g., *Journal of the American Forensic Association, Journal of Sociology, New England Journal of Medicine*)

2. National newspapers and news magazines (e.g., the *Wall Street Journal, Christian Science Monitor, Time, Newsweek*)

3. Regional newspapers and news magazines (e.g., the *Chicago Tribune, Atlanta Constitution*). A regional source, dealing with a regional issue, can potentially be perceived as having more credibility than a national source dealing with the same issue.

4. Local newspapers and news magazines (e.g., the *Journal Star, Pekin Times*). A local source, dealing with a local issue, can be perceived as having more credibility than either a national source or a regional source.

5. Specialty publications/sources—those targeted at specific groups of readers divided by interest, gender, race, etc. (e.g., *Ladies Home Journal, Ebony, Car and Driver*, Internet sites). The credibility of specialty publications/sources is greatest within their target groups and much less outside those groups. However, when a speaker is dealing with a topic that encompasses the target group, these specialty sources increase greatly in credibility with all groups.

6. One-time publications. These have lower lower credibility than the preceding sources since they usually are not updated or are updated less frequently than the other sources (e.g., books, videotapes, audiotapes).

Second is the *test of competency*. The purpose of this test is to make sure that the source is truly competent, which means being trained and/or experienced in the area where he or she is being used as a source. Sources have limited competency. For example, though a doctor, a podiatrist would not be a competent source for a speech on open-heart surgery. Titles do not necessarily confer competency. In fact, choosing a source because of his or her title can often introduce the grapevine effect into the situation. Politicians are a good example. Although the information used in their speeches may have come initially from a competent source, it reaches the politicians indirectly through their staffs of researchers and speechwriters.

The *test of prejudice* is third. Though no source is totally free from prejudice, a speaker should definitely avoid obviously prejudiced sources—those with a vested interest in the outcome of whatever is being discussed, which could cast significant doubts on the credibility of information from the source (e.g., an anti–gun control speech citing the National Rifle Association).

Fourth is the *test of verifiability*, whose purpose is to make sure that any information used by a speaker can be verified by any listener who chooses to do so. Thus, an interview with an undercover police officer on gangs would likely be a good source. However, if the officer asks you not to use his or her name, you have a major problem in terms of *ethos.* There would be no way for the listeners to verify the information. Did the interview really take place? Did the officer really say those things? Unnamed and unverifiable sources generate too much doubt to be used by a speaker.

Fifth, the test of *statistical soundness* can help both speakers and listeners make better choices concerning statistical information. This final test is divided into four parts.

1. A speaker should make sure that the statistical information being used has been classified accurately. *Accurate classification* deals with the statistical relationship between sample and population. The speaker needs to make sure that the sample is truly representative of the population. The population is the group that the statistical study wants to gain information about, and it is usually a very large group. Since most populations are too large for statistical study, a subgroup of the population is used. This subgroup is called a *sample*, and the results obtained from the sample are considered to be true of the entire population. Still, if the sample was not truly representative of the population, the results would not be valid.

2. A speaker should make sure that an *adequate sample size* was used for the statistical manipulation. Logicians, as opposed to statisticians, believe that reliability is tied to sample size. For them, perfect statistical results can only be achieved by using the entire population. Further, logicians believe, as the sample gets smaller, the reliability of the results is reduced.

3. There should be *significant results.* Although speakers tend to present statistics selectively, a wise speaker should know what all the numbers represent before using them. The same would apply to a wise listener before accepting them.

4. A *reasonable sampling process* should be employed. A speaker should make sure that the sample was not constructed to bias or predetermine the results. A stratified random sample or a representative random sample puts together a sample that demographically mirrors the population being studied. Using such a sample improves the statistical reliability of the results.

The preceding information should help you conduct research and develop credible content for your presentations.

Communication Situations: Enhancing a Presentation

If you are doing a speech on tarantulas, a live one (once you get past the screams and hysterics generated by arachnophobia) might be a very good visual aid. For a speech on model trains, your Lionel circa 1960 (after the hassle of packing it up, worrying about lost or broken parts, and reassembling it) might also be very effective. However, you can save a lot of time, effort, and worry by putting together a PowerPoint presentation to accompany the speech.

When used properly, PowerPoint can greatly enhance a presentation. As the speaker speaks, visual, sound, and color changes can keep the average listener engaged. One key idea for any speaker to remember is that a PowerPoint presentation is for the audience, not for the speaker. PowerPoint should not be treated as a giant set of speaker notes. Another key idea for speakers to remember is that PowerPoint is used differently in a teaching/learning situation than in a general speaking situation. In most speaking situations, a series of relevant pictures continually looped can act like background music; they serve to keep the audience engaged. Let's examine some structural basics for PowerPoint.

© The Gallery Collection/Corbis

Why Are Pictures Better than Words?

Under most normal circumstances, a PowerPoint presentation should consist of only pictures/visuals or these and a few words. A PowerPoint presentation consisting of words alone rarely succeeds in holding an audience's attention. Always remember that you can say the words but, keeping television in mind, the pictures may be the key to holding the audience's attention. A UCLA study indicates that a visual/graphic PowerPoint presentation is five times as likely as a word-oriented PowerPoint presentation to be remembered.

The pictures chosen should visually enhance or more fully explain what is being said. They should be easily visible to the audience and clearly related to the subject. Animated images, cartoons, photographs, and symbols can play a very useful role in a competent PowerPoint presentation. All of these visuals can likely be stretched so that they fill the screen completely or almost completely. However, be careful when resizing the pictures; you do not want to create visuals that are grainy and unclear. One of the best introductory speeches that I have ever seen had only pictures of the speaker at various stages of his life, and those pictures clearly mirrored what was being said about him.

Words should be used very sparingly in a PowerPoint presentation. In general, the presentation should include key words or key phrases only when they are crucial, and should be accompanied by a compelling, compatible visual image. Make sure that the focus is placed on the visual elements and not on the words. Sometimes, when exactness is needed, a powerful quotation along with a image works well, but where absolutely necessary, key words and phrases can be used. These words or phrases should be viewed from the audience's standpoint. In other words, key words and phrases, along with the visual image, should be necessary and should be designed to help the audience better understand and remember the essence of the presentation.

When words are used, they should be more than just words. They, too, should be a part of the visual effort to hold the audience's attention. Animate the words. Give them entrances, exits, and emphases that will enhance their visual appeal and carry them far beyond a stagnant and minor contribution to the presentation's success. If you are giving a talk on the common housefly and the word fly appears on the screen, let the word actually fly around as a real housefly would.

Why Are Font and Color Selection Important?

If the PowerPoint presentation is not visually appealing to the audience, it does not increase the speaker's *ethos* with the audience. Even elements such as font and color play important roles. When choosing a font, first take a look at what is available to you. Most word processing programs today provide several options; even more fonts can often be downloaded from several online systems. Second, try the font out. Don't guess; take a look and make an actual evaluation. Will that font be easily readable by any audience member? Font size can be adjusted to fit the PowerPoint frames as well as for readability. Speakers frequently have to toy with font size and type until they get what is best for the audience.

Background color and font color can aid or hinder a speaker's success. PowerPoint comes with a series of background frames. If they are used, the speaker has to make sure that other visual elements and fonts will fit. The speaker must also ensure that the selected font color doesn't lose visual prominence on the background frames. Speakers can choose a blank frame. PowerPoint allows them to set the frame up as they wish and even provides tools to help them do so. Color can be added to the frames from a reasonably full selection of colors provided by PowerPoint. Again, color selection should be such that all of the frame's elements work together for the best audience impact.

How Can the Use of Sound Effects, Video Clips, and Powerpoint Animation Improve a Presentation?

Even the best speakers cannot use vocal variations, gesticulation, and movement often enough to hold the audience's attention. Along with the other elements of PowerPoint, sound, video, and animation help keep the audience engaged.

PowerPoint comes with an array of sound effects, and others can be downloaded or added from various sound effect CDs. Sounds effects should be varied, should be used with restraint, and should not overwhelm the speaker's vocal efforts. Sound effects may work best to alert the audience to visual changes in the PowerPoint slides and in the speaker's points or ideas. Sometimes sound can be used to set or enhance the mood that the speaker is trying to create. Experimenting with various sounds is the best way to figure out what works.

PowerPoint also allows for the animated use of words and pictures. An animated PowerPoint slide helps to hold the audience's attention. It is possible (but difficult) to construct a slide with too much animation. When this happens, it is the slide and not the speaker that becomes the focus of audience attention. Due to the relatively low listening abilities of the average audience, a good deal of animation may be necessary to help the audience focus. Some pictures or clips (available on PowerPoint or downloaded) are already fully animated. Like the picture, the animation should be relevant to the speaker's message.

Relevant video clips can also be used. There are two issues to be aware of here. First, make sure that you can actually add the video clip and make it work. You must pretest it before your presentation. Second, make sure that the video clip is brief. If the clip becomes the focus of the presentation, the speaker will seem superfluous in the minds of the audience. Don't use the clip to set itself up; this is probably the most common reason why clips end up being too long. Set up the clip and preview its content before showing it.

PowerPoint gives a speaker various animation schemes that can makes words and pictures/graphics move, and can even make slide transitions an effective visual element of the presentation. Since PowerPoint allows the speaker to control slide transitions, you will have to decide how you want to move from slide to slide by trying out the various methods first. Using different transitions each time there are slide changes enhances the

speaker's ability to hold the audience's attention. These slide transitions add to the visual impact of the PowerPoint presentation.

This brings us to the general question of how the slides for the PowerPoint presentation should be advanced. There are two choices. Slides can be advanced singly by the speaker or set to advance after a designated passage of time.

The decision is not complicated. If a speaker's goal is to instruct, then single advancement of slides may be preferred. This speaker has to make sure that the listeners can perceive the information, understand it, and retain it. Matching the pictures with the words is extremely important.

However, if the speaker's purpose is other than instructional, timed advancement is likely a better option. The speaker does not have to worry about advancing the slides, which happens automatically, but does have to make sure that there are enough slides so that the pictures don't end before the message is completed. Generally speaking, it is usually better for timed presentations to be looped. A looped presentation gets to the last slide and simply begins again. This prevents the presentation from ending visually before it has ended verbally. Still, the speaker has to have plenty of pictures to make the looping effective. With too few pictures the looping would become repetitive, making PowerPoint a liability to the presentation rather than an asset.

Should I Use a Floppy Disc, a CD, or a Flash Drive to Store My Presentation?

Choosing a means of storing your PowerPoint presentation depends more on where it will be used than on any other factor. The limitations of the presentation location may limit your choice of storage methods. If the computer equipment of the presentation space accommodates only one form of storage, your choice is predetermined. Do you know what the presentation space will allow you to use? All three forms—floppy dis, CD, and flash drive—are competent storage methods; let's explore them. The floppy disc is a good method for storing some PowerPoint presentations. However, many presentations exceed the available space on a floppy disc, and discs are easily corrupted. When using the floppy disc for storage, always carry at least one backup disc as well. For your credibility as a speaker, it is always better to be safe than sorry. Here is a useful hint: keep your floppy away from your cell phone and other electronic devices.

The CD is a great way of storing a PowerPoint presentation, but if you do not have a CD writer that allows you to put your presentation on a CD, it is useless. If the presentation space does not have a computer with a CD drive, the CD is also useless. CDs can host several PowerPoint presentations effortlessly, but some computer systems take a while to load such presentations. Also, over time, CDs can get scratched. If a CD is used regularly, it is a good idea to have a backup. (In fact, it is always a good idea to have a backup.)

The most recently developed storage device is the flash/jump drive. Like CDs, flash drives can hold more, As with CDs, if your computer is not equipped for them, they would be useless. Make sure that you have a flash drive that is compatible with the system you will be using. Checking in advance will prevent you from erring.

Outside the classroom, there is also the possibility of pulling up you presentation from your own remote website. Often this creates a time boondoggle because you have to find the site, load it, and find the presentation and load it. There is always a chance that the protection software of the presentation computer will not allow you to access the site. This is why it is not permitted in the classroom setting.

Now, since you have some information, you can make a more informed choice about how to store your presentation.

What Should I Know about Plagiarism and Copyright?

© Lou Oates, 2009. Used under license from Shutterstock, Inc.

Borrowing the ideas or words of another person or source without giving them credit is illegal, unethical, and prohibited. The unauthorized use of visual images is also prohibited. If the visual image is copyrighted, you cannot use it unless you have permission. For example, if you were making a presentation on Caterpillar, you could not go to the Caterpillar website and just take their logo to use. You would have committed an illegal act by violating their copyright. Most (but not all) of the time, sending an email request to the webmaster explaining how and why you want to use the website's visual image may result in permission to use the image. Following is some very general information about copyrights and the use of copyrighted material.

Copyright law covers this and more:

- Fiction and nonfiction, including books, periodicals, manuscripts, computer programs, manuals, film, audiotapes, and computer disks

- Photographs, prints and art reproductions, maps, charts, technical drawings, diagrams, and models

- Slides/tapes, multimedia presentations, filmstrips, films, and videos

- Records, tapes, cassettes, and computer disks

Copyrighted works may be used with these conditions as guidelines

- If a work belongs to the public as a whole (public domain, e.g., government documents and works, items with an expired copyright, and works published over 75 years ago)

- If one has received prior approval for the proposed use by the copyright owner

- A parody of a copyrighted work would be exempt

- Generally speaking, that which is used for educational purposes; however, there are restrictions

Luckily, there are many sites providing free images that you can use for your presentations. You can always find specific picture types (which do not have copyright restrictions) by conducting an Internet search. This is another reason to begin researching your presentation early rather than at the last minute.

Why Should the Presentation Space Be tested?

A competent speaker almost never makes a presentation of any kind without testing the limits of the presentation space. Seating, lighting, and acoustics can all play a very important role in speaker success. Some of the elements a speaker may not control, but the speaker should understand and be able to adapt to all of them. Here are some questions to ponder:

- Can the speaker use all of the equipment effectively? If not, is there someone who can show the speaker how to do so?

- Does the seating allow for a clear view of the speaker and the PowerPoint presentation?

- If necessary, can seating adjustments be made?

- Does the room's lighting enhance or detract from the speaker or the PowerPoint presentation?

- If necessary, can lighting adjustments be made?

- Do the acoustics of the room require vocal volume adjustments from the speaker?

- If necessary, how does the speaker ensure that all audience can hear the presentation?

- Do the acoustics of the room require sound adjustments for the PowerPoint presentation?

- How does the speaker make sure that the sound is adjusted properly?

- Does the available LCD projection system change the PowerPoint presentation's effectiveness?

- What adjustments can be made to the PowerPoint to maximize its impact in this performance venue?

- Should the slides be advanced one by one or should they be looped to have the best audience impact?

Richland, L. Bjork, R, and Finley, J. *Lonking Cognitive Science to Education. 2005 Annual Conference of the Cognitive Science Society.*

Communication Situations: Persuasive Messages

Persuasion can be like the punch you never see coming, and because you did not see it coming, it ends up having a strong effect on you. Persuaders like politicians and advertisers are busy throwing those punches; are you wise enough to see them coming? The only way to guarantee that you are not affected by the punches (unless you want to be affected) is to know as much as or more about persuasion that the persuader does.

What is *persuasion*? In its simplest terms, persuasion is manipulation. Manipulation of what, you might ask? Persuasion is the manipulation of attitudes. Why would you manipulate attitudes? Persuasion is the manipulation of attitudes for the purpose of controlling behavior. Persuasion has behavioral change as its terminal goal. That behavioral change could be getting you to buy a product, to vote for a candidate, or even to riot in the streets.

Since persuasion is the manipulation of attitudes, understanding attitudes is necessary to a fuller understanding of persuasion. An *attitude* is a disposition to react favorably or unfavorably to something. This definition leaves little or no room for the neutral attitude. It indicates that the only way not to have an attitude is to have a total absence of information. Once information is obtained, you would have a natural proclivity to react favorably or unfavorably to it. Sometimes, our disposition produces an attitude that is so weak that our conscious mind isn't aware of it. At other times, our disposition produces a very strong reaction of which our conscious mind is quite aware.

Courtesy of Catholic Online

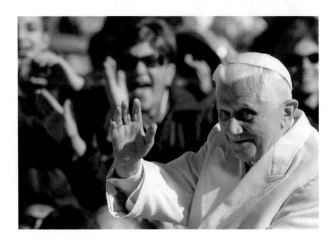

Every attitude has three basic components: a cognitive component, an affective component, and a behavioral component. The *cognitive component* deals with two diverse elements: that which is logical and that which seems logical but isn't. Something that seems reasonable at first glance but not after careful examination is called *pseudologic.* Thus, the cognitive component can be driven by either logic or pseudologic. The cognitive component is an independent component; that is, how we think can be independent of how we feel. The *affective component* is the emotional side of an attitude and deals with how we feel. Like the cognitive component, the affective component is independent. How we feel can be separate from how we think. The *behavioral component* consists of our actions or reactions to something. It is this final component that the persuader hopes to control. The behavioral component, however, is a dependent component. It depends on how we think and/or feel.

When the cognitive component and the affective component have the same valence (positive or negative), it is easy to predict the behavior of a mentally healthy person. We think vegetables are good for us, for example, and we like the taste of vegetables. Thus, we will eat vegetables. As long as the two valences remain the same, the behavior will remain the same. The situation in which the cognitive and affective components have the same valence is known as *classical alignment*. To change the behavior, you would have to change the valence of one or both components. When the valence of the cognitive component is different from the valence of the affective component, the stronger valence will determine behavior. For example, if we think vegetables are good for us but we do not like their taste, whether or not we eat them will depend upon the valence strength of each component. If the cognitive component is stronger, we will eat vegetables. If the affective component is stronger, we will not. When the valences of the cognitive and affect components are different from one another, the situation is known as *nonclassical alignment*.

It isn't enough just to understand the components of an attitude. You also have to know its characteristics. The characteristics of an attitude generate attitudinal difference and make you aware that not every attitude can be manipulated in exactly the same way. Here are the five characteristics of an attitude:

- *Intensity* is the relative strength of an attitude. Various attitude scales can be used to show how strong or weak an attitude is. The stronger the attitude is in opposition to the behavior you want to evoke, the more difficult persuasion will be. By comparison, weak opposing attitudes make persuasion easier.

- *Dominancy* is the centrality of an attitude to the person's entire value system. The core attitudes (a sense of good/bad, right/wrong, and religious convictions) are at the center of our being, with all of our other attitudes to some extent connected to or dependent upon this core. Core attitudes are sometimes called *foundation attitudes* or *dominant attitudes*. In normal rhetorical situations, these core attitudes are virtually immune to persuasion. Trying to convince someone with a different viewpoint about abortion, euthanasia, or the death penalty to behave as you want them to behave would be an exercise in futility. The person's entire value system would have to be changed to embrace the new attitude; this happens only on television or in the movies. In the real world, core or dominant attitudes are among the best-protected entities on the planet. We remain very consistent in terms of what we believe to be right or wrong, good or bad.

- *Salience* is the awareness of an attitude. If we are consciously aware of an attitude we hold, it is said to be salient. However, attitudes that we are not consciously aware that we hold (nonsalient) are also virtually immune to persuasion. You cannot manipulate an attitude that is not acknowledged.

- *Direction* of an attitude means that it is moving away from the no-attitude zero point on an attitude scale and is getting stronger. An attitude that is moving toward the zero point on an attitude scale is getting weaker. Nonetheless, these are not instantaneous events. It will take a series of encounters between persuader and persuadee over a period of time to strengthen or weaker an attitude. Obviously, it will take more time to weaker and/or destroy an existing attitude than it will to strengthen an existing attitude. Except in movies and on television, one persuasive speech will not change the world.

- *Stability* is really habit. Humans are creatures of habit, and they get accustomed to thinking, feeling, and behaving in particular ways. When attitudes are not subject to persuasion, they tend to grow more stable. We get set in our ways. The more stable an attitude is, the more difficult it will be to manipulate it (exception: it will be relatively easy to reinforce that attitude).

If you understand the characteristics of an attitude, you can develop a more successful approach to manipulating it. Some attitudes are highly influenced by only one characteristic and other attitudes by multiple characteristics. Being able to identify and analyze each attitude change situation smooths the road to behavioral change.

Courtesy of Hillary Clinton Campaign Office

One final critical piece of information about attitudes deals with their formation. Where do attitudes come from? Attitudes are formed based on three factors: an environmental factor, a self-interest factor, and an internal consistency factor.

Have you noticed that in most cases that your attitudes are not far removed from those of your parents or other primary caregivers? Our foundation attitudes are formed when we are young, and our *home environment* contributes significantly to this process. Our neighborhoods, our schools, and our churches contribute to the process as well, but none of them have the constant access that can be found in the home. We formulate or emulate a sense of good/bad and right/wrong at home. And remember, all of our other attitudes may be dependent upon that core that we develop. Though we may go through a period of seeming to reject those home attitudes to establish our own autonomy and individuality, we end up remarkably similar to our early caregivers. Trying to institute a behavioral change that would be rejected by the environment is extremely difficult. As long as the persuadee recognizes the conflict, the attitudinal manipulation will not be successful. However, if the attitudinal manipulation could be made to seem consistent with the environment, the manipulation might work as long as the disconnect was not recognized.

The *self-interest factor* recognizes that a mentally healthy person would not knowingly embrace a new attitude if that attitude is harmful. We embrace attitudes that help us. Once again, though, if the persuader can make the persuadee believe that an attitude is helpful when it isn't, the manipulation will be successful until the persuadee recognizes the disconnect.

The *internal consistency factor* tells us that no mentally healthy person will embrace a new attitude that conflicts with already existing attitudes. To do so would generate *dissonance*, defined as internal tension and turmoil. Humans do not desire a dissonant state and will maneuver to avoid it. Yet, if a persuader can make a persuadee believe that the new attitude is consistent with other existing attitudes even when it isn't, the manipulation may be successful.

At this point, dissonance needs a bit more explanation. Dissonance is necessary to motivate behavioral change. If the persuadee believes that things are fine the way they are, then there is no motive for a behavioral change. If, on the other hand, the persuadee exists in a dissonant state, then he or she has a motive for a behavioral change to try to reduce or eliminate the dissonance.

With dissonance in mind, let's take a look at some serious obstacles to persuasive success. Chief among these obstacles are the selective triplets: selective exposure, selective, perception, and selective retention. The selective triplets have as their goal the protection of our attitudes, especially our core or dominant system of attitudes. The selective triplets are subconsciously controlled; their functioning is automatic. The best advice to give a persuader is to avoid triggering this defense system because once it is triggered, persuasion will fail. The selective triplets can be triggered by an attack on the core or dominant system or by an excessive use of dissonance. Think of this defense system as you would a mine field. Knowing how to navigate it can get you closer to your goal.

The selective triplets represent a three-tier defense system. If a persuader gets past selective exposure, then selective perception steps in to defend. If a persuader gets past selective perception, then selective exposure steps in to defend. Nobody gets past selective retention; thus, persuasion would fail. Let's examine each of the selective triplets:

- *Selective exposure* is the natural tendency to avoid anything or anyone who creates dissonance for us. The higher the level of dissonance, the stronger the avoidance response will be. You don't have to think about it; it happens naturally. For example, some students feel dissonance due to the necessity to take a math class or a communication class. They avoid the classes and even avoid thinking about them until they are forced to do otherwise.

- *Selective perception* is the ability to see only what we want to see and hear only what we want to hear. Generally speaking, dissonance can't pierce this veil and neither can most persuaders. Have you ever had a discussion with a friend or an acquaintance whose constant tactic is to turn virtually everything that you say into support for his or her position? If you have, you have dealt with someone protecting the self with selective perception. Like selective exposure, selective perception happens automatically.

- *Selective retention* awaits anyone who is lucky enough to get past selective exposure and selective perception. Selective retention is the final stop on the track to derailing persuasion. If something creates too much dissonance for us, we simply erase it from memory. We cannot be affected by what we cannot remember. For example, if there is someone in your family whom you would like to stop smoking, do not yell, "You're going to die, going to die, going to die!" That would create excessive dissonance, and the message would be expunged from memory. Each time the message is placed in memory, it would also be erased. Every time the smoker lights up, the negative smoking data does not run through his or her head. Instead, it is like that data never existed.

The other two obstacles are rookie persuader mistakes—having no action step and having a weak advocative attitude.

An *action step* is typically unique to persuasion; it comes at the end of the persuasive message, and it serves as a dissonance relief valve. If the persuader has generated enough dissonance to merit a behavioral change, the persuadees need to know specifically what behavioral change is required. Is the behavioral change as simple as purchasing the advocated produce, or is more required? Action steps come in two varieties. There are *active* action steps, where the primary responsibility rest with the audience, and *passive* action steps, which depend mainly on the persuader. Action steps should meet a standard of reasonableness for the society in which they are presented. In the United States, advocating voting out the politician is more reasonable than advocating blowing up the politician. As an example of an active action step, let's say that a persuader has generated enough dissonance to make an audience believe that a stop sign at the corner of Baker and Bassett Streets would be a good thing. What behaviors can the persuader advocate that will achieve this? It would be reasonable if the persuader asked the audience to write letters of complaint to the local department of transportation. In some cases, sending a text would be more appropriate. An email, a fax, or a phone call might be the best option. It is important that the persuader choose one option to advocate rather than a scattered approach that might confuse the audience. Once an option has been chosen, the persuader needs to give audience all the essential contact information. If you have asked them to write a letter, provide the mailing address. If you have asked them to send a fax, provide the fax number. If you have asked them to send an email, provide the email address. If you have asked them to make a phone call, provide that number. Though you do not provide a word-for-word message, you should give the audience an idea of what must be communicated. Finally, set a deadline by which you want this behavior to be demonstrated. The deadline should underline the urgency of the situation but should be reasonable. A fourteen-day deadline would be best. Without a deadline, behavioral change is highly unlikely.

Active action steps provide longevity in terms of manipulation, but they may not produce widespread behavioral change. If the persuader desires large numbers of responses and is willing to settle for lack of longevity, a passive action step could be used. The most common passive action form is the petition. If the petition is used, the persuader should draft a professional-looking document. Before the petition is given to the audience, its content should be read into the record. This preempts the boondoggle of each audience member reading and analyzing the document before deciding whether or not to sign.

Here's a little trick. If the first person who gets the petition signs it, there is peer pressure on others to sign as well. Carefully consider who will get the petition first.

The final obstacle to the process of persuasion is also an error on the part of the persuader. It is a weak advocative attitude. An *advocative attitude* is the demonstrated force of advocacy. In other words, persuaders should both look and sound as if they believe what they are saying. Subtlety is not highly prized here. If a persuader does not look and sound like a believer, it will be almost impossible to convince an audience to accept and believe.

Since attitudes have both a cognitive and an affective component, we need tools that will help us manipulate each set of components. Let's begin with *pathos,* or the emotional side of an attitude. A speaker can develop and use basic motive appeals. The top five motive appeals come from Maslow's hierarchy of values, which deals with what are often called the *basic human needs.* However, we shall call them what they are to communicators—*motive appeals.* If speakers utilize these motive appeals by subtly promising the rewards associated with them, then they can probably evoke the desired response from the listener. The *physiological motive appeal* deals with basic necessities such as food, water, sleep, and sex. To achieve the desired effect with this motive appeal, the speaker should subtly promise that more of these desired necessities will come from acting as the speaker wants or accepting his or her point of view. Earlier American politicians used phrases like "a chicken in every pot." Though it lacked subtlety, it was effective in getting votes. Today, the message is one of "no new taxes," which subtly promises that one will have more money for food and other necessities. Although to Maslow sex meant species preservation, modern advertisers have stretched the idea to mean individual gratification. Initially, products like perfumes and colognes made the buyer sexy. Today, most products seem to make the buyer sexy. From toothpaste to breath mints and gum, the list keeps growing. However, outside of the product arena, this expanded use of Maslow's hierarchy rarely appears. Presumably, ideas and philosophical positions do not hold a believable promise of sex appeal.

After 9–11, the *safety motive appeal* grew in its ability to shade perceptions. Here the speaker's rhetoric promises safety to those who take the action he or she advocates. In today's world, an idea that promises safety from terrorism would likely be embraced. For decades in the United States, the idea of keeping oneself and one's family safe has generated success for both political parties, which routinely promise that a vote for them "keeps guns off the streets," "keeps the criminals in jail," and "keep drugs away from our children." Automobile manufacturers, tire manufacturers, and insurance companies routinely use the safety motive appeal to pitch their products.

The third of Maslow's five motive appeals is *belongingness.* This motive appeal works by employing the promises of group identity and affection. It is common for employers to sell the ideas of wage or benefit cuts by talking about the *corporate family* and what's best for it. On college campuses, the terms *brother* and *sister* draw men and women to fraternities and sororities. Most organizations use some form of belongingness to attract members.

The *esteem motive appeal* works by promising recognition, respect, and/or envy. Today, claiming that an idea has special moral or ethical value is a way to sell it. People who embrace the idea believe that they will be respected and/or envied by others because of their "high moral ground" or "high ethical standards." In other words, taking the action or accepting the idea makes them special compared to others. Having the right products can also generate respect and envy. From Nike to Lamborghini, special people are sold special products that make them better than the rest.

Finally, there is Maslow's *self-actualization motive appeal*. This is the promise that one can move from what one is currently to what one ultimately aspires to be. It is all about hope, wish, and dream fulfillment. As an example, consider ideas involving education or educational reform. A strongly held idea in American society is that an education can take one from poverty to wealth and fame. These promises, both subtle and not so subtle, are not necessarily valid or reasonable, but they can get people to embrace or buy into ideas attached to them. The army slogan "Be all that you can be" is the epitome of self-actualization.

A speaker who can put together the right words and nonwords can likely get listeners to see things his or her way. These motive appeals and tactical devices manipulate an audience by evoking an emotional response and distorting their perceptions of reality. There is another way of employing Maslow's motive appeals. A speaker's rhetoric can threaten to take away one or more of these essentials. That threat, if not excessive, can also emotionally manipulate and inspire action on the part of the listener. A speaker who promises an audience more of Maslow's basic needs if they do as he or she asks is using what is called the *fulfillment approach*. By contrast, the threat to take away Maslow's essentials if the audience doesn't do as the speaker wants is called the *deprivation approach*.

Like Maslow's hierarchy, Leon Festinger's *cognitive dissonance theory* can be applied to persuasive manipulation. Festinger suggested that everyone exists primarily in one of two states of existence. One state, called *consonance,* is the absence of internal tension and turmoil. Consonance is the desired state of mentally healthy human beings. However, as long as a person is in a consonant state, persuasion is neither desirable nor possible. The other state, called *dissonance*, is characterized by the presence of internal tension and turmoil. Dissonance is not a desirable state. It makes persuasion both desirable and possible.

To structure a persuasive appeal for a dissonant audience, a persuader suggests that if audience members do as he or she asks, dissonance with be reduced or eliminated. With a consonant audience, an extra step is required. First, the persuader must generate dissonance. Everything has a flaw. The persuader finds the flaw and chips away at it until he or she has generated sufficient dissonance to motivate a desire for behavioral change. Then the persuader promises the audience that if they do as he or she asks, their dissonance will be reduced or eliminated.

Benjamin Whorf and Edward Sapir probably had no idea that their work would generate such discussion and debate. What came from their work is called the *Sapir-Whorf hypothesis*, which explains how language (both verbal and nonverbal codes) can be used by a speaker to restructure the audience's perception of reality. Thus, we shall spend some time describing communication's ability to reshape the reality of listeners. Let's continue our examination of the tactics that can be used to manipulate the listener's emotions. Persuaders will often use these tactics to tap into the emotions of the audience.

The first tactic is known as the *rustic myth*. Using this myth, the speaker casts himself or herself as the simple but wise old sage and recounts a proven story or adage designed to stimulate an emotional response. The nature of the story or adage depends upon which emotion the speaker is attempting to manipulate. The story of the Abraham Lincoln studying by lamp light could be used to inspire dedication as an example.

The second device is called *strive for success*. Like the rustic myth, this device uses a narrative form. However, this narrative form is limited to stories of people overcoming obstacles to achieve great success. The purpose is to inspire people to work toward the goal of success. The story of Michael Jordan's initially failing to make the basketball team and his continued efforts that led to his success would be inspirational.

The third tactic, known as the *greater reward,* has its roots in the Judeo-Christian ethic. It is all about reminding people that if they endure their current troubles, there will be a greater reward at some future point. Choosing the right words to convey this message as well as using the best cadence/pace of delivery is essential in evoking the desired emotional response. If you examine Martin Luther King's "I Have a Dream" speech, you will find elements of this tactic there.

© Betmann/Corbis

The fourth device, called *fight the conspiracy,* works by provoking anger against a common enemy. The enemy is demonized and held responsible for an overt negative reality. Union leaders demonize companies, political parties demonize each other, and politicians currently demonize terrorists. The final desired impact is anger against the enemy and alignment with the speaker, leading hopefully to some desired action.

The third nonnarrative device and the fifth device overall is known as *take the challenge.* The speaker sets goals for the listeners and ties these goals to the human egocentric nature. By telling the audience that only certain kinds of people can reach these goals (e.g., those who are intelligent, hard-working, creative, resourceful), the speaker sets up a situation whereby the ego is forced to prove itself by attaining the goal.

The third narrative device and the sixth device overall is called *personification.* The purpose of this device is to "put a face" on the situation. The story of one person is told with strong emotion in great detail. These stories can be used to evoke myriad emotions from an audience. Charitable organizations use this tactic frequently to provoke people to donate money or to volunteer their time.

The seventh device, known as *symbolic persuasion,* uses symbols to manipulate emotions. The American flag is almost always present when the U.S. president speaks. The purpose is to subconsciously trigger a patriotic response. The atmosphere effect uses artifacts and can be used in conjunction with most of the other devices. Here the term *artifact* refers to visual representations such as pictures, symbols, and banners. Getting just the right visual is essential in making any of these devices work most effectively. Here are a few examples. If the focus of fight the conspiracy were the tobacco companies, the use of the "no smoking" logo would be appropriate. If the focus of take the challenge was a rededication to the space program, pictures of our solar system and of various space vehicles. If the focus of personification was the Children's Federation, pictures of a child in dire poverty would be appropriate.

The *big lie,* the eighth device, is exactly what it says. When you tell a small lie or medium-sized lie, there is room for doubt. The dichotomy becomes: either it is true or it is not true. Whenever a big lie is used, the dichotomy shifts. Either it is true or they think I am dumb enough to believe it. Our egocentric nature often has us swallowing the lie. Con artists use the big lie on a regular basis, and many are quite successful. Consider, for example, the con known as the *pigeon drop*. Here, money is allegedly found by the con woman. She becomes hysterical and doesn't know what to do. She pulls in a passerby and shows the bag of money that has allegedly been found. Their conversation and the con woman's continued hysteria pull in the con woman's partner, who advises her to hold the money for thirty days, at which time it becomes hers. The hysteria returns when the first con woman realizes that both of the other women know about the money and could claim it. A plan is devised whereby all three will allegedly share in the found money. A substantial deposit must be put down by the second con woman and the passerby. Contact information is shared. And, at the end of the thirty days, the two women will get their deposits back, and all will share in the found money. In reality, the plan all along was for the two con women to walk away with the passerby's cash. Unfortunately, this con works all too well and all too often. The big lie does raise an ethical/moral question. Only your ethical/moral standards can determine if it is a viable device for you as a speaker. I am not advocating that people lie, but, without knowledge, this could be the punch you don't see coming.

The final device, called the *scapegoat technique*, can be used by a persuader who has an audience at a high level of dissonance (natural or generated). The dissonance level needs to be high but below that detected by the selective triplets. Because the scapegoat technique preys on so many human frailties and because it may require the sacrifice of the safety of innocent people, it is a particularly heinous device. This one really pushes the moral/ethical envelope. People experiencing a high level of internal tension and turmoil have a natural tendency toward *projection*, the need to blame others. They want to find someone who is responsible for the state in which they find themselves. All the persuader has to do is to suggest someone to blame; great salesmanship is not required to make this work. The persuader will suggest confrontation with the scapegoat. Unfortunately, all the pent-up frustration and hostility spill out and are aimed at the scapegoat.

Relief from dissonance follows; the persuader has saved the day. The persuadees, however, will find themselves trapped in an endless feedback loop. Little by little, the persuader will ask them to do things. Because the persuadees feels that they owe a debt to the persuader, they will comply. Little things will become bigger things. Of course, you are probably thinking that the persuadees can stop anytime they wish, but they cannot. To reject the persuader at this point would mean confronting and embracing the guilt over what had been done to the scapegoat. Humans will do incredible things to avoid guilt. Hitler rose to power principally because of his use of the scapegoat technique; today the same technique is used to recruit gang members. See if you can figure out how that works.

A mistake made by novice public speakers is to burden a speech with too many devices. It is best to select one or two tactics and use them in a well-developed, carefully thought-out manner.

With tools in hand that will help you manipulate the affective component, it is now time to turn our attention to the cognitive component. The art of argument does not depend on who can scream the loudest or on who can talk the longest. The art of argument, to be effective, depends on *logos*. *Logos* is the ability to generate understanding with regard to the statements that a speaker is making. To bring clarity to those statements, a speaker needs to know how to structure an argument. In order to make sure that you know how to structure an argument properly, we will begin by examining Stephen Toulmin's model.

© Betmann/Corbis

89

The Toulmin model is a rhetorical-logical model. Unlike the once popular Aristotelian model, the Toulmin model allows the speaker to state the degree of certainty or probability associated with his or her argument, and it clearly shows the relationship of all the components of the reasoning process to one another. The Toulmin model consists of six parts: the claim, the evidence, the warrant, the qualifier, the reservation, and the backing for the warrant. We shall examine each of them.

The *claim* is the assertion or conclusion made by the speaker; it is what he or she wants to prove or have the listeners accept. Claims are made on the basis of evidence, and they generally fall into one of four categories—designative, definitive, evaluative, and actuative.

A *designative* claim deals with questions of fact—whether or not something is true. Here are some examples of designative claims: "Byron Howell, the defendant, committed the murder." "The U.S. is experiencing an economic decline." "Television has an adverse effect on children."

A *definitive* claim deals with questions of definition, and the argument centers on whether or not something meets the definitional standard. With the argumentative definitional term underlined, here are some examples of definitive claims: "A quota system is not <u>democratic</u>." "College hate speech rules infringe on the <u>freedom of speech</u>." "Debra Howell's statements are <u>slanderous</u>."

An *evaluative* claim deals with questions of value—whether or not there is merit to something. Here are some examples of evaluative claims: "The college curriculum is not relevant to or good for today's students." "College entrance exams no longer serve a correct and useful purpose."

An *actuative* claim deals with questions of policy—whether or not something should be done. Your persuasive speech should be an actuative claim. Here are some examples of actuative claims: "The electoral college should be abandoned as a means of electing the president." "Schools should install metal detectors as a means of reducing school violence." "Elderly drivers should be tested yearly to reduce the potential for accidents."

No matter what kind of claim the speaker makes, the speaker's argument should be sound. Whenever a speaker makes a claim, he or she has the responsibility to demonstrate that the claim is justifiable.

The second part of Toulmin's model is *evidence.* Evidence is extremely important to the speaker; it determines the soundness of the speaker's claim. For a fuller discussion of evidence, you should review Chapter 10, which discusses the types of evidence that a speaker can use. The speaker should examine all available evidence—not only evidence that can be conveniently located or evidence supporting his or her claim.

The *warrant*, the third part of the Toulmin model, is the link between the evidence and the claim. It is the reason why the claim is considered credible; it is the basic premise upon which the claim rests.

The fourth part of the Toulmin model is the *qualifier*, which expresses the degree of certainty that can be attached to the claim. Since speakers rarely have absolute certainty about any claim, words such as *most likely, probably*, and *presumably* are useful in helping the speaker qualify the claim.

The *reservation*, the fifth part of the Toulmin model, identifies the circumstances under which the claim would be null and void. The reservation is one of the reasons why a speaker should be aware of evidence that does not support his or her claim. The reservation is not expressed as a part of the speech, but the speaker should know what the reservation is and that it is false.

Finally, there is *backing for the warrant*, which consists of evidence and reasoning designed to make the warrant credible and reasonable to the listener.

Let's put all of the parts together so that you can see how the Toulmin model works.

CLAIM: The U.S. prison system should (*probably*) be reformed.
(*Qualifier*)

EVIDENCE: FBI crime statistics indicate that violent crime is on the rise.

WARRANT: Prisons are not rehabilitating those who are released early, paroled, or finish their sentences.

BACKING FOR WARRANT: A Department of Justice report indicated that prisons are not rehabilitating criminals. The recidivism rate shows that we are not rehabilitating criminals.

RESERVATION: The claim is true unless most of the violent crime is committed by first offenders.

Now that you have some idea of how the Toulmin model works, we will move on to specific forms of reasoning; there are five of them. The first form of reasoning is *reasoning by generalization*. This involves making observations and drawing conclusions from those observations. However, conclusions from this form of reasoning must pass three efficacy tests. The observations must be representative or common, the number of observations must be logically sufficient, and exceptions must be recognized. Consider the following example; are the efficacy tests met?

For the last year, we have traversed the lower forty-eight states observing birds. We have observed birds under virtually every circumstance imaginable. At the end of the year, one member of our group tells us that, based on her observations, she has concluded that most nondomesticated birds tend to fly in southerly directions as the months grow colder.

The second form of reasoning is *reasoning by analogy*, which means to reason by making comparisons. For the conclusions stemming from this form of reasoning to be valid, they need to meet two efficacy tests. First, the speaker should make sure that the two items being compared are specifically alike and not just generally alike. Comparing apples and oranges doesn't work logically because they are only generally alike; both are fruit. Comparing oranges and tangerines does work because the two are specifically alike; both are citrus fruit. A craving for an orange probably would not be satisfied by an apple, but the craving probably would be satisfied by a tangerine. Second, the speaker has to account for circumstances that might occur and invalidate the comparison.

Reasoning by causal relationships is the third form of reasoning. This form of reasoning is sometimes called *regressive* because it moves backward to its conclusion. Reasoning by causal relationships is based on the cause–effect situation. One begins with the effect and works backward to discern its causes. Though there are both major and minor causes for any effect, there is no one cause to one effect. The direct cause–effect relationship (one cause to one effect) seemingly does not exist. There are four efficacy tests with this form of reasoning. The speaker must make sure that he or she has not confused cause with coincidence, has not confused sufficient cause with immediate cause, has eliminated the possibility of intervening variables, and has accounted for contributing variables.

The fourth form of reasoning is *sign reasoning*. This occurs when one event is used as an indication of another event. For example, from inside our homes, when we see the leaves on the trees rustle, we assume that the wind is blowing even though we cannot see or feel the wind. Sign reasoning, to a great extent, is based on past experiences; it is one of the weakest forms of reasoning. The efficacy tests for this form of reasoning include differentiating between accidental (a squirrel causing the leaves on trees to rustle) and coincidental (wind causing the leaves on trees to rustle) relationships, checking for reciprocity (leaves don't rustle when wind isn't blowing), distinguishing between special (an earthquake causing leaves on trees to rustle) and normal (wind causing leaves on trees to rustle) relationships, and discovering collaboration (flags also rustle when leaves do).

Finally, there is *reasoning by circumstantial detail*. This form of reasoning occurs whenever a speaker draws a conclusion from a particular pattern formed by a series of events. Multiple conclusions can be drawn from the same pattern. To meet the efficacy tests here, a speaker must be able to show that the series of events does fit the pattern and that the conclusion he or she draws from the pattern has the least amount of uncertainty attached to it. For example, a series of events discovered by police detectives may fit the pattern of homicide. The prosecutor may conclude that the pattern proves that the accused, Byron Howell, committed the crime. The defense attorney may use the same pattern to conclude that the defendant, Byron Howell, did not commit the crime. The conclusion that has the least uncertainty will be accepted by the jury as being valid.

In addition to the forms of reasoning, a speaker needs to be aware of some special argumentative forms—reductio ad absurdum, cost-benefit analysis, and risk-benefit analysis.

Reductio ad absurdum means to reduce to the absurd. This rhetorical device is used to help speakers overcome the impact of fallacies. Though not logical, fallacies often seem reasonable. Listeners often accept false rhetoric, and it becomes difficult to get them to see the folly of the conclusion. Reductio ad absurdum can be used to reduce the illogical conclusion to its illogical extremes and help the listeners see how ridiculous the conclusion really is. Sometimes this device's use is necessary to erode illogical ideas that have been erroneously accepted as true over time or accepted due to popular support.

Cost-benefit analysis is used only when the benefits are guaranteed; it weights the costs (the negatives) of a particular action against its benefits (the positives). If an action has more benefits than costs, it is deemed reasonable. If an action has more costs than benefits, it is considered less reasonable. If there are examples of a particular solution that is truly similar to your own, working somewhere comparably, then this is the argument to use.

Risk-benefit analysis is used with untried solutions where the benefits are only potential and not guaranteed. Like the cost-benefit argument, the risk-benefit argument weighs the risks (the negatives) of a particular action against the benefits (the positives). Any action generating more risks than benefits is not deemed viable. New ideas and solutions, which have never been tried before, should be subjected to a risk-benefit analysis.

We have briefly considered logic, which can drive the cognitive component, but pseudologic can also motive this component. Thus, we should spend some time talking about pseudologic, or the fallacies of reasoning. By the strictest definition, a *fallacy* is a mistake or error in the chain or pattern of reasoning. Fallacies are pseudologic or false logic. Some fallacies are committed accidentally/unintentionally, but others are committed intentionally by the speaker. Since pseudologic may seem reasonable to the average listener, a speaker can use fallacies to deceive the audience. Whether or not a speaker should knowingly employ fallacies to achieve his or her goals is an ethical question. However, a listener who understands the fallacies can guard against being deceived.

Following are the twenty-three most commonly committed fallacies and a rhetorical device used to combat the deception of a fallacy:

The fallacy of *non sequitur* (translation = it does not follow) is committed when a speaker moves from premise to conclusion without explaining the route taken. Consider the following example: "It is raining outside; therefore, I will bake a cake." The problem is that the speaker failed to explain how he or she got to the conclusion. Had the speaker said that it was raining outside? He or she had a list of chores to do, all of which required being outdoors except for baking the cake; therefore, he or she will bake a cake.

A speaker who uses conclusionary statements in an attempt to sneak a point with no substantiation past the audience commits the fallacy of *begging the question*. The rules of logic require that proof be presented before conclusions are drawn. This fallacy is most often committed in the oral preview statement, where often conclusions are drawn without the presentation of prior proof. (Preview Statement example: "Let's discuss the evils and horrors of nuclear power plants.")

The fallacy of *circular reasoning* is committed by a speaker who uses two unproven statements to justify each other. In reality, no proof has been presented, but it may seem to many that it was. It is a more rhetorical version of the old why/because game: "Why? Because. Because why? Just because!" If the speaker is clever enough, he or she may be able to make the audience see proof when none exists.

The fallacy of *shifting the burden* (*ad ignorantiam* = to ignorance) violates the Aristotelian concept that "He who asserts must prove." Instead of proving whatever he or she wants the audience to accept, the speaker will challenge the audience to disprove it. Due to an audience's passive nature, no one will interrupt and many will assume that because the statement wasn't disproven, it must be true. (Example: "There is no reason why marijuana should not be legalized in this country, and I dare you to show me otherwise.")

The fallacy of *irrelevancy* should be easy to spot because the speaker tells the audience that something isn't relevant when in fact it is. This is a way of getting an audience to put aside ideas that might work against the speaker's purpose. (Example: "A discussion of the cost of converting our electricity production to solar power really isn't relevant to discussing the possible full-scale use of solar power.")

The fallacy of *overstatement* is committed whenever the speaker uses exaggeration. Though exaggeration seems to be a natural part of how we communicate (in the special case of persuasion), it could be used by the audience to deny all of the speaker's logical points. (Example: "There are a million reasons why we should adopt a policy of isolationism.")

The fallacy of *hasty generalization* is committed whenever a speaker draws a conclusion without having enough observations upon which to reasonably base that conclusion. Example: Whenever someone says that women are bad drivers, have enough female drivers in relation to the total population of licensed female drivers in this country been observed by the speaker? Our culture abounds in hasty generalizations. "Blacks are shiftless," "Mexicans are lazy," "Native Americans are stoic," "Chinese are inscrutable," and "Jews are stingy" are just a few of the many examples of this fallacy.

The fallacy of the *absolute* (*dicto simplicter*) is the most commonly committed fallacy. It is easily committed because our language gives us the words and phrases to produce all-inclusive generalizations (*all of you, each and every one of us*, etc.). All the listener need do is to find one exception to the rule; the listener can then use that example to deny everything that was said.

The fallacy of *damning the origin* (*ad hominem*) is committed whenever a speaker only gives you the source's lack of credibility as a rationale for rejecting information. Logically, if information should be disbelieved, there should be a way of reasonably explaining that to the audience. (Example: "You cannot believe that information about the CIA; after all, it was given by the liberal media.")

The fallacy of the *ipse dixit* (translation = he said it himself) is just the opposite of damning the origin. Here the speaker tells the audience that they must believe something simply because of the source of the information. Again, logic dictates that other rationales should be present. (Example: "You have to believe that; it was printed in the *New York Times*.")

The fallacy *ad verecundiam*, or the famous fallacy, is committed when speakers substitute well-known people for expert sources. (Example: "Matt Damon says 'Vote for candidate X in the upcoming election.'")

The fallacy *ad populum* (translation = to the populace/majority) is committed whenever the speaker tries to make statistics absolute proof of a point. The numbers, the audience is told, mean that the point is absolutely true. (Example: "Since the opinion polls show that most Americans are opposed to affirmative action, then we should abandon that policy.")

The fallacy of the *false analogy* (false comparison) is committed by speakers who compare two things that are only generally alike and are not specifically enough alike to allow for a valid conclusion to be drawn from their comparison. For example, consider the idea that Sweden has a mandatory seatbelt law that saves lives, so the United States should have one as well. Though Sweden and the United States are both countries, the comparison is not valid concerning the ideas that most affect traffic safety because here the two countries are radically different from one another.

The fallacy of the *false dilemma* (if . . . then "reasoning") is committed by speakers who try to construct false absolute situations. In logic, an absolute situation is expressed in the "if . . . then" form. When the "if" part of the statement occurs, the "then" part must automatically, without exception, follow. Logic recognizes few absolutes. Speakers sometimes try to make the audience believe in an absolute bad thing following an action or lack of action. This threat of some sort of doom is designed to manipulate audience behavior. (Example: "If you vote for candidate X, then you will wind up with higher taxes.")

The fallacy of the *false dichotomy* (either . . . or "reasoning") is committed by a speaker who attempts to make the audience believe that their only choices are among two undesirables. This is done to make the audience choose the lesser of two evils, which is the choice that the speaker wanted the audience to make all along; the speaker got them to do so by making them believe that the only other choice was worse. Other choices do exist, but the speaker camouflages this situation. (Example: "Either you are for freedom of speech or you are a communist.")

The fallacy of the *red herring* is committed whenever a speaker throws the audience off the listening track in an effort to sneak something past them; it is much like trying to throw bloodhounds off the scent by dragging herring around behind you. Sometimes the speaker simply throws an emotionally charged element into the mix to distract the audience; at other times, the speaker uses a verbal/nonverbal strategy to achieve the goal of distraction. In stage one, the speaker tells the audience that he or she is going to prove something. In stage two, the speaker begins a long, disorganized speech. Remember listener frustration? The point here is that the speaker is trying to prevent the audience from listening effectively. In stage three, the speaker uses some nonverbal tactic to regain the audience's attention and then draws a conclusion without ever presenting a shred of proof. Many listeners will accept the conclusion, believing that the proof was presented when they were not attentive.

The fallacy of the *straw man* is committed by a speaker who so narrows the scope of his or her topic (to the exclusion of all the other issues) that it becomes impossible to disagree with the speaker. The fallacy is that broad issues cannot reasonably be reduced to a single point. (Example: If a speaker opposed to gun control told you that the only fact you needed to consider in deciding the issue was that 12,000 children died each year due to handguns accidents, he or she would be committing the fallacy of the straw man.)

A speaker who commits the fallacy of *tradition* tries to use tradition as a logical justification. To tell someone that something is reasonable because that is the way it has always been is not logical. (Example: "We have always used these teaching methods; therefore, we should continue to use them. Don't fix something unless it is broken.")

The fallacy of *composition* is committed when a speaker tells the audience that what he or she knows or can prove about the parts must be true of the whole as well (composition – parts = whole). (Example: "I read a study that said that some college students might cheat on tests, so college students as a whole should not be trusted.")

The fallacy of *division* is the opposite of the fallacy of composition. Here the speaker tries to tell the audience that what he or she knows or can prove about the whole must also be true of the individual parts (division – whole = parts). (Example: "Since you are a Catholic, you must be against artificial means of birth control.")

The fallacy *ad misericordiam* is committed by speakers who attempt to substitute emotional justification where logical justification is required in an attempt to milk sympathy and empathy. (Example: "I know that I haven't done the work for this class, but you can't flunk me. I have had problems this semester. My girlfriend dumped me, I wrecked my car, and I've been depressed.")

The fallacy of the *hypothesis contrary to fact* is committed whenever a speaker draws a conclusion based on events that did not occur. Essentially, the speaker rhetorically alters the past and bases his or her conclusion on that alteration. Since all the variables that might have interceded to impact the situation cannot be accounted for, any one conclusion drawn from a supposition is not the only possible conclusion that could be drawn. (Example: "If I had just studied two more hours for that exam, I would have gotten a better grade.")

The fallacy of *mistaken cause* (*post hoc ergo propter hoc*) can be committed in two different ways. It can be committed by a speaker who tries to claim that one thing and one thing only is the cause of something, or it can be committed by a speaker who confuses cause with coincidence. The first way is usually intentional and designed to deceive the listener. The second way is usually unintentional. (Intentional Example: "Violent video games are the cause of violence among our youth.") (Unintentional Example: "I found a four-leaf clover; therefore, I will have a good day.")

Communication is part art and part science. It merits further study by anyone who wants to improve his or her communication skills. Understanding the tools used in effective communication and understanding the potential pitfalls when communicating are both parts of the process. Work at it. Good communication skills will always serve you well, from dealing with friends to spouses and from home to the boardroom. Good luck and good communicating!

© Tim Pannell/Corbis